BECOME A MILLIONAIRE FOR WHAT IT MAKES OF YOU!

"WISHING YOU SUCCESS IN ALL YOUR ENDEAVORS"

Pierre Lautischer

By Pierre E. Lautischer

The information in this book is true and complete to the best
of the author's knowledge. All recommendations, advice and
concepts are made without guarantee on the part of the
author or Piemar Promotions Ltd. The author and publisher
disclaim any liability in connection with the use of this
information.

Library and Archives Canada Cataloguing in
Publication

Lautischer, Pierre E. (Pierre Eric), 1958-
Become a millionaire for what it makes of you! / by
Pierre E. Lautischer.

ISBN 978-0-9917316-0-2

1. Finance, Personal. 2. Wealth. 3. Well-being. I. Title.

HG179.L38 2012   332.024'01   C2012-906900-0

1st Edition - 2nd Printing

PRINTED IN CANADA BY BLITZPRINT INC.

This book is dedicated to the love of my

life, Marla. "Ma Pierre"

And my sons, Christopher and Corey,

act on your ideas and anything is

possible.

Acknowledgements

When undertaking any kind of project there are always many people that will help you along the way. Some may even be unaware of what they have provided. To all my silent mentors including the likes of "Jim Rohn", "Zig Ziglar", "Robert Kiyosaki", "Napoleon Hill", "Tom Hopkins" and many more. Thank you for providing me the countless hours of materials to study and philosophies that helped me get where I am today. Hopefully, this work will pay it forward and others will benefit from reading it.

My mother-in law, "Lois Walker", who believed in me, provided positive feedback and spent many hours correcting my mistakes by proof reading the book. I could not have done it <u>correctly</u> without you.

"David Schrader", a friend who unknowingly provided me the inspiration to complete this book. He allowed me to read the beginning of <u>his</u> book and this challenged me to complete mine.

Preface

In this day and age, becoming a "Millionaire" is still a lofty goal and it has never been easier. To be labeled as such, an individual requires a net worth of at least one million dollars. That is, total assets (real estate, stocks, bonds, cash etc.) less total liabilities (loans, mortgages, credit card balances etc.). The primary goal of this work is to help those interested in helping themselves.

So how is this different from any other financial book? It focuses both on techniques to become wealthy and to elevate one's character. Most of the information presented is based on both the author's financial history and readings.

Use of the principles and concepts described, will hasten your journey to prosperity. Does this mean that when these principles are put into action, no mistakes will occur? Unfortunately no, but they will assist in diminishing the number of learning experiences (failures). Plan to win by considering this book as your reference template and create your own personal plan.

Each chapter is devoted to a specific idea. You are sure to recognize some of these topics, as they are based on old philosophies. Please take your time reading. Dissect each chapter by highlighting relevant thoughts and making notes in the margins. At the end of most chapters, you will receive an action list. These are meant to further your knowledge base and provide you with experience.

This is the first of a series and is meant to serve as an introduction. Each subsequent work will expound on the ideas presented. The language used is fairly simple but use a dictionary for unfamiliar words, as this will give the passages more clarity. It is the author's sincere wish that you are able to use this book to help yourself to becoming financially independent, enhance your life and the lives of those around you.

Table of Contents

Chapter One – "I" Chapter

This first chapter is known as the "I" chapter and details my plight from having a negative net worth to over a million in approximately six years. I don't like to air my dirty laundry, but I do want you to see the obstacles I had to overcome to get where I am today. My hope is that you will have an easier time than I did and that perhaps reading this book will make that possible.

The lowest point in my financial history occurred in December 2000 when I had to declare personal bankruptcy. It was embarrassing, stressful and ruined my credit for seven years. Although, this is a traumatic event, it provided a valuable learning experience and the knowledge I gained will be promulgated to you later. Try to avoid getting to the point where bankruptcy becomes an option. Those who unfortunately have been through it will be able to relate as I try to describe what it is like.

You start with these small debts that eat away your resources or income, like small garter snakes. Then as they get bigger, you think you can control them, perhaps by combining them into a line of credit. These small snakes are consumed by a much bigger one like an anaconda, which starts to wrap itself around your legs. The anaconda (debt load) increases in size and begins slithering further up your body. With the passage of time, it completely wraps you with just your head exposed and out of the blue a major financial event occurs.

You are now being smothered by the debt and with no other way out you need someone to cut this thing off. The snake cutter, bankruptcy, destroys reputations and any business dealings you've built. Then, for at least seven years, you're credit is ruined as no financial institution will touch you.

*Avoid bankruptcy anyway you can, start early by managing your debt and try not to live above your means!

How did I get in this mess? Let me tell you! I was a Peace Officer making reasonable money and my wife at the time, was a stay at home Mom running a family day home. Although we had a reasonable amount of money coming in, we had very little in savings and were living above our means. We purchased an expensive home with the help of a big mortgage. We ate out all the time and I was leasing my brand new SUV. Of course I needed to exercise the line of credit by buying a corvette that was driven maybe once a week.

At the time of all this spending, our marriage was breaking down. I should have seen the writing on the wall, but instead we spent more. Then in 1998 we separated, my ex took what little we had in the bank accounts and I was left to look after both boys and all the bills. I had two maxed out lines of credit, a mortgage and credit cards to juggle (juggling means using one debt paying for another). I was unable to save any money and if anything major came along, I would be finished.

That major thing occurred and my estranged wife sued me for interim spousal support and was awarded $1000 a month. I had to oblige the courts but between looking after the boys, maxed out debt and zero savings there was no money to pay it. So, in December 2000, owing more debt than I had in assets, I declared bankruptcy.

At the time, I was bitter towards my ex, but little did I know that she had done me a fantastic favor. For it was at this time, that I turned my financial future around. I realized that I would not be financially independent unless I was able to find other ways to increase my wealth. So I began studying diligently looking for ways to get to my goal of being a millionaire. Financially, I could not do anything except study and plan during the period of bankruptcy.

November of 2001, I was discharged from the bankruptcy and was finally able to begin the climb to financial independence. Using most of the principles, techniques and philosophies in the chapters that follow, I went from a negative net worth (more liabilities than assets) in 2000 to having over a million net worth by July 2007. If I can do this during the seven year period of post bankruptcy, you can do it as well.

At the end of each chapter, you find a summary and a work list, most of which I would like you to complete before moving on to the next chapter. The discipline of following the work list will not only make you wealthier but will also develop your personality and change your mind set. The following chapter discusses the key ingredient to become a success and is required if you want to become a millionaire.

Chapter Two – Action

Action is defined as the act of doing something, it can be positive or negative, but is required if you want to become wealthy. 95% of people fail as a result of not even taking the first step. Without action, I would still be trying to recover from my bankruptcy and would not be where I am today. Jack Canfield (Co-author of Chicken Soup for the Soul series) said, "Everything you want is out there waiting for you to ask. Everything you want also wants you. But you have to take action to get it."

Fear is one of the greatest deterrents to action, whether it is fear of failure, fear of the unknown or fear of rejection. A great part of fear can be overcome by education and experience. By reading this book, you are overcoming fear through education. Doing the action lists at the end of the chapters will provide you with experience and in turn reduce your fears.

Also, fear can be reduced through the law of numbers or averages. For example, going to a high school dance and asking someone to dance. A lot of people will not even ask someone to dance because of the fear of rejection. What is the worst that can happen? They will say no. Did you have someone to dance with before you asked? No, do you have someone to dance with now? No, then ask someone else, it is a numbers game and eventually someone will say yes! A helpful acronym for F.E.A.R. is False Evidence Appearing Real.

This is good time to introduce the Pareto Principle which describes the law of averages and defines the 80/20 ratio. What it means is that 20% will do 80% of the work and 80% will do 20% of the work. We can break it down this way, only 20% of the people who buy this book will apply the principles. Make sure you are part of that 20% and give it that honest effort.

The good news is you have already taken action by obtaining this book and reading it. Let's continue this positive action by reading the rest of book and actually implementing the ideas you will be exposed to.

What has this got to do with wealth creation? If you do not try, as in "take action", you will never succeed. "You will always miss 100% of the shots, you do not take" Wayne Gretzky #99. Throughout this book you will be asked to take action, your success depends on it.

Do you want to be wealthy? Do you want to know that your kids and their kids will never have to worry about money? Do you want to quit working for someone else? Do you want to retire early? Do you want to own a Ferrari? Do you want to live in a mansion and/or travel the world? Would you like to support your favorite charities? All of this is possible, if you have the desire to make it happen.

Desire is the starting point, because desire activates motivation, which is the beginning of action. If you want something bad enough, you will overcome any obstacles in the way to get to it. Remember the example depicted in chapter one of overcoming the obstacle of bankruptcy to achieve wealth. Think about what you want, right here and now. It is the time to make changes in your life. Do it for yourself, the people around you and those you want to help.

Chapter Summary

Without action you will not become wealthy. Even if you were to win a lottery, you still have to take action to buy a ticket and search for the winning numbers. Five percent of the population will retire wealthy, do you want to be included? If you wish to be wealthy you must have the desire to do so and the willingness to work to get there (action).

Get a piece of paper and a pencil and get ready to write. Your success will be determined by this action point. If you want to be wealthy, setting goals will go a long way to streamlining your progress.

Chapter Three – Goals

A quote from Brian Tracy (Motivational Speaker and Author), "All successful people; men and women are big dreamers. They imagine what their future could be, ideal in every respect, and then they work every day toward their distant vision, that goal or purpose." There are many different ways of determining and setting goals. What follows is a simple and easy way to get started. We will expand on this format in future books, but for now let's go through this condensed format.

First, <u>write down</u> at least 4 ten-year goals and keep in mind what you desire and what it will require to achieve those goals. There is no maximum number of goals you can list, but to keep focused start with 4. You will have the opportunity to update and add to your goals list later. When you are ready to commit thoughts to paper, think big! On your piece of paper, write down the date exactly ten years from today and your goals. Next to those goals, write down why you want to achieve those goals.

Listed below is an example:

1) December 31, 2023 Net Worth of $1,000,000

I want to provide my family with piece of mind and have no worries about the future.

2) December 31, 2023 *Passive Income of $8000 a month

This amount will keep me comfortable without having to work. *(Passive Income is money that is generated by investments or businesses, not having to work for it)

3) December 31, 2023 Bank Balance of $50,000

This will provide peace of mind by knowing that I have a liquid emergency fund for anything that comes up.

4) December 31, 2023 Travel to Austria for a month

Go to where my parents were born to visit relatives and expand my horizons.

Once you have completed your list, read it every night before going to sleep and in the morning when you wake up. This constant reinforcement, will program your mind not only to see your goals but also instill the belief that you can achieve them.

Short-term goals are merely the measurable steps that it will take to get to those long-term goals and are usually set out annually on specific dates. Create a table documenting the annual figures that you will require to get to your ten year goal. Add an extra column, so you can plot the date that you achieved the annual goal. Not only will you see your short-term goals but also your progress.

Using our previous example of obtaining one million net worth in ten years, it would be easy to calculate one million divided by ten years and obtaining short term goals of one hundred thousand per year. Each reader will have different goals and starting points, so using the above formula is unrealistic. Below is a table which can be can used for our example and can be adjusted to meet your specifications.

Date	Amount	Date Achieved
December 31, 2013	$0	Dec. 31, 2013
December 31, 2014	$50,000	
December 31, 2015	$125,000	
December 31, 2016	$200,000	
December 31, 2017	$300,000	
December 31, 2018	$400,000	
December 31, 2019	$525,000	
December 31, 2020	$650,000	
December 31, 2021	$775,000	
December 31, 2022	$900,000	
December 31, 2023	**$1,025,000**	

As you progress through those ten years, you will update these goals to reflect your successes. You may achieve goals earlier or have substantially more than you estimated. You can now adjust either the dates or amounts to reflect your success. (In other words, decrease the ten year date or increase the amount of net worth on the original ten year date).

The above chart only lists the first of our ten year goals, it is possible to chart the rest of our goals using the same dates and just changing the amounts. For instance the big trip to Austria, figure out how much it will cost and start <u>saving</u> specifically for that purpose. Breaking down each year and/or splitting it into 3, 5 and 10 years. 3 and 5 year goals are actually mid-term goals.

You can see that breaking down your goals to bite size chunks makes attaining them that much easier. Want some really good news? Most of you will have some net worth already and your starting point will be above the zero mark. This enables you to either increase your goals or shorten the time span. Never adjust your goals by extending dates or reducing goal amounts. Should it happen that you don't make your yearly goal by the set date, then use this to motivate you further to achieve next year's goal early. For those of you with a negative net worth, there is still hope, remember where the author's been.

While we are on the topic, right now you are going to replace one word in your vocabulary. From now on, you are not to use the word, "Failure" because there is no such thing. You will replace it with "Learning Experience", if used correctly or positively you will learn more from this than any book can provide. Although this is the toughest way to educate yourself (school of hard knocks), it will stick with you for life. Every self-made millionaire has had their share of learning experiences and they have recognized the power of turning them into positive events. Divorce, bankruptcy and business collapse are learning experiences the author has personally gone through. Try to learn from others experiences. Your task is to try to avoid these types of experiences and yet to embrace them if they happen. Get something out of it, by figuring out what you did right and what you did wrong.

If you are truly interested in becoming wealthy, before you go on to the next chapter, write out your goals. Once you have them down on paper, review them every night before you go to sleep and continuously update them. When you have achieved any goal, celebrate your success and replace it with a bigger and better goal.

Chapter Summary

This chapter looked at goal setting and by using it you will streamline the process to wealth. Remember this is not a get rich quick scheme. You will have to work smart and put time in to realize your goals.

So let's get started, below is your action list from this chapter;
1. List your 10 year goals and describe the reason why you want to achieve them.
2. Chart your 10 year goals breaking them down to yearly increments,

which we will call your short term
goals.

3. Review your goals **list** every day just
   before you go to sleep.
4. Make this declaration every morning
   when you arise: from Tom Hopkins
   (Sales Great, Author and
   Motivational Speaker), "When I fail, I
   will only look at what I did right."

We explored setting goals and
becoming a millionaire, that's fine and dandy
but how are we going to get there? The next
chapter talks about one of the techniques that
will help to get you there.

Chapter Four – Pay Yourself First

It's not how much you make, but it's what you do with what you make that makes the difference. "Pay Yourself First" is a very old philosophy and is just as relevant today as it was yesterday. Most if not all wealthy people, use this concept in one form or another. The author has and still uses this technique successfully.

What is Pay Yourself First? It is pretty well a definition within itself. Anytime you receive any money, from any source, the first person you pay is yourself. Your bills, your groceries, your obligations, your entertainment expenses all get paid after you pay yourself.

Now where you start will be determined by your goals and personal situation. A common starting percentage and incredibly easy to calculate is 10%. So if you were to get a $1000 net paycheck (meaning take home pay) you would set aside $100 for the "Pay Yourself First Fund". Some calculate this amount on their gross pay (that is before deductions) and some cannot manage 10% to begin with so they start with 5 or as little as 1%. What is important is to start and once things work out you should increase your percentage. If you find that you are in later stages of life, you may have to start at a higher percentage. It really depends on the goals you have set for yourself. For you younger readers, the good news is that time is on your side and starting at 10% will allow you to amass a fortune.

Taking 10% will affect your spending patterns, but soon you will become used to working with the balance remaining. As your situation improves, so does your percentage. For instance, you start with 10% and in two years time your debt has been reduced and your cash flow has improved, you then go to 20%. As your financial picture improves you increase the percentage paid to yourself.

The next point is the most important part of the Pay Yourself First technique. **You are not allowed to access the funds for anything other than investment purposes!** You will be tempted to use it for getting that boat you always wanted or you may find yourself short on grocery money and promise to pay it back, **NO!** This money is for your future. At some point you will be able to use the money that comes from this source but not until the pot is so great that your withdrawals will be miniscule in comparison.

You will require a parking spot for the fund, so find the bank account that pays the best interest rate and does not charge you for transactions. Later, if you are lucky enough to find an investment that provides a higher growth rate, you will be further ahead to transfer the funds to that account. All investment accounts can be fed with monthly or lump sum transfers from the parking spot you have set up.

This "Pay Yourself First" fund is going to take a tremendous amount of discipline on your part. Set up an envelope at home and mark it "PYF". You will place the portion of cash into this envelope until you can physically deposit money into your parking spot. Making the deposits electronically is even better, by transferring from the account in which you receive the money, to your PYF account. The best way to do this is to have the bank <u>automatically</u> make the percentage transfers when any money is deposited. By automating the process, there will be less opportunity to spend the money before it gets into the account.

Regardless of which method you choose, it will take discipline to make consistent deposits. You will be amazed at how quickly funds will accumulate.

Chapter Summary

"Pay Yourself First" gives you a starting point on the road to wealth. At first, it will be easy to contribute to this fund but as it continues to grow you must resist the temptation to use the funds for other purposes. This fund is specifically for wealth creation and not to be spent on other things. Just as with goals, you must continually update the percentage you are contributing.

Below is your action list from this chapter;

1. Determine what percentage you will be able to start with. Keep in mind your current financial status, goals and stage in life.
2. Find a financial institution that provides a high interest account with no charges and set up an account.
3. Set up any electronic arrangements for transfers and/or electronic transfers to this new account.
4. Do you have money sitting elsewhere to kick start this account? Then by all means place it in the PYF account. Before you do, make sure that the PYF has a better growth rate. That is the interest earned is higher than what you are getting now.

Remember this account is merely a parking space until we find a better investment or use for the money. There are a couple of preliminary items to consider before we look at generating wealth.

Chapter Five – Wills and Life Insurance

Both wills and life insurance provide peace of mind. Setting up a will is important, as it allows you to bequeath your assets according to your wishes. Without one, the estate holds all the assets and the government will then distribute assets using their own formulas. This process can last for years. By setting up a will, division of assets will occur timely and to your specifications. It is relatively cheap to obtain a will and to make sure that it is properly executed, use a lawyer to set it up. Even if you don't have assets now, you will later. Strive to update your will at least once every two years.

Life insurance also provides peace of mind. Although contrary to popular belief, it's not for everyone. What is life insurance for? Everyone would like to think that they will live forever, but there are two things in life that are certain, death and taxes. While we may try to minimize taxes we will never avoid death. The purpose of insurance is to support those we leave behind. If you are single or have no dependants, you may not need life insurance. Life insurance can have other uses but we will only be concerned with the description above. With that being said, always buy term insurance. It provides the cheapest premium and with the proper amount of coverage will provide your loved ones with the needed support. Avoid other insurance products such as whole life and universal life which provide insurance and investments combined. These policies tend to be extremely expensive.

How much coverage do you need? That truly depends on your circumstances, age and current income. Generally, enough to cover replacement of your income to the day you could have retired. So if you are making $50,000 a year, are 45 years of age and intended to retire at age 60 you would need $50,000 a year times 15 years ($750,000). Other variables exist such as current interest rate, amount of debt being carried etc. that will affect the amount of coverage required. These are not exact figures and the advice of a professional insurance agent should be sought when determining how much coverage to get. Don't forget your spouse or common-law, they may also require coverage should something happen to them.

There may be a certain time in your life where life insurance may no longer be required. An example of this may be when you are financially independent and most of your income is passive. This can happen for someone who is wealthy or someone who has retired and has paid off all their obligations (mortgage etc.) and receiving ample retirement income. You also may determine you are at a point where you require less coverage. This is why when buying term it is important to select the right term, 20 and 25 years are the most common. As the term increases so does the premium.

If you already have life insurance, make sure it is term insurance. If it isn't, see your insurance agent and discuss options with them. If they are unwilling to offer a term product then seek a second opinion. If you do not have life insurance and do have dependants that look to you for support, you can consider using a portion of your PYF to finance the premiums. Although, it is suggested that you fund the life insurance premiums from outside of the PYF fund.

Chapter Summary

A will provides for the distribution of your assets in accordance with your wishes and is done in a timely manner. Life insurance provides for your dependants when you can't. Always buy term insurance as it is the cheapest and will provide you piece of mind.

Below is your action list from this chapter;
1. Obtain a will through a lawyer.
2. Determine whether you require life insurance.
3. Locate a professional insurance agent.
4. Buy term insurance.
5. Try to fund premiums for insurance from outside of your PYF account.

There are a number of building blocks to getting your financial house in order. Wills and Life insurance are just two of the steps. Another one is the establishment of an emergency fund which will be discussed in the next chapter.

Chapter Six – Emergency Fund

Like Life Insurance, the establishment of an emergency fund will provide peace of mind and is yet another building block of a solid financial house. An emergency fund should be kept and used exclusively for expenses and outlays that occur unexpectedly. Examples include the loss of a job or income where expenses still need to be paid. Another example could be an unforeseen outlay such as the replacement of a furnace. Anytime money is used from this fund, your first priority is to replace that money.

How much should the emergency fund contain? This is a hot topic among financial planners, but it will depend on you and your particular situation. It is usually based on covering a number of months of your expenses. A simpler way is to assess whether your income covers your expenses and if so look to replace your income for 3 – 6 months. The more you have slated for emergency purposes, the better your peace of mind, although too much will become an opportunity cost (money you lose by investing in something with a lower growth rate). Let's say you have an income of $5000 per month, therefore to cover 3 to 6 months, the emergency fund should have $15,000 to $30,000 in it.

How do you accumulate that kind of money? One alternative is to use a percentage of your monthly PYF money until you have what you feel is sufficient. If you have kick started your PYF then apply all your kick start monies. Going back to the example above, if you are contributing $500 a month to your PYF, then using $250 a month or 50% to set up the emergency is reasonable.

How should we park the emergency fund money? Continuing our example, always keep at least one to two months in <u>cash</u> ($5,000 to $10,000) and then the remaining balance should be placed in a liquid, higher growth investment. Higher growth, meaning you are making more money than you are getting in the PYF account and liquid enough that you should be able to cash out the investment in less than two weeks. Liquid means that funds can be converted to cash quickly whereas growth refers to the amount of return generated (usually expressed as a percentage). Ideally this investment should be a fairly low risk product (depending on your tolerance). We will be discussing Risk and Risk Tolerance in future chapters.

There is no need to set up another account, as long as you can track how much is allocated to the emergency portion. As for what to invest in, you should research what best suits your needs, but with limited knowledge in investing, look towards investments that are professionally managed such as mutual funds, segregated funds and ETFs. Note that ETFs (Exchange Traded Funds) have very low management fees and are traded on the stock exchange. There is such a variety of each of these that you should find something that provides the liquidity, growth and safety (risk) for emergency money. A future chapter on Mutual Funds, Segregated Funds and ETFs will provide a detailed description of each.

Some believe that a line of credit or credit cards can serve as an emergency fund. As you will see in a later chapter on credit, use of credit for an emergency fund creates bad credit. Credit you are trying to avoid. Anytime you use credit to purchase consumer goods or pay for expenses it is termed as bad credit. Usually it is expensive (credit cards are in the 20%+ interest rate range) and you set up liabilities instead of assets. When you set up an emergency fund, you set up an asset and it puts money in your pocket. There is such a thing as good credit and we will explore that later.

Chapter Summary

An emergency fund sets aside cash to cover unexpected loss of income or expenses that arise. It should be about 3 – 6 months of money to cover income or expenses for the same time period. Once you have one to two months worth of cash, invest the remainder in higher growth, liquid, low risk investments.

Below is your action list from this chapter;

1. Considering your circumstances, determine how much your emergency fund should be.
2. Determine how much of your "PYF" will be used to establish the fund.
3. Once you get close to the cash limit, begin looking into investments for the remainder of the funds.

So now you have set your mind at ease by considering obtaining a will, life insurance and setting up an emergency fund. You may have found some good investments for the remainder of your funds, but let's wait until you have read the next chapter on the various investments and subsequent chapters detailing those investments.

Chapter Seven – Investments

This chapter discusses what to do with the remaining money from your PYF. A quick reminder, any money designated in your PYF fund or any growth generated from that money stays in the fund and cannot be used for anything else other than investment purposes. You may come across excess cash which you would like to place in the PYF, this is great and will catapult you to meeting your goals, but remember once it is in there it cannot come out unless being used for investing. The same applies to increasing the percentage you contribute every month or week, once you raise it, you can't lower it.

There are many areas where money can be invested and the following is just a partial list. An investor who is just starting out should restrict themselves to those investments that are managed by professionals such as mutual funds, segregated funds, and ETFs. When you buy into these, you are pooling your money with others to buy companies usually listed on stock exchanges. Some of these funds provide income back to the investors in the form of dividends and/or interest, while almost all these investments provide growth in the form of capital gains.

Since we are on the topic, let's define the three types of income that investments produce. The three types are interest income, dividend income and capital gains. Capital gains are the difference between what price you bought the investment for originally and what you sold it for or its value today. For you sharp readers, yes that does mean you could have a capital loss. Dividend income is a distribution of the profits from companies forwarded to the owners of the company. Finally, interest is paid out by companies, governments and institutions as a result of you lending money to them.

Stock investing is the purchase of shares in a specific company, in other words ownership of the company. Bonds involve lending money to various organizations and receiving interest in return. The most common investments in Real Estate include buying properties for the purpose of rental income, flipping or speculation. We will discuss stock investing, bonds and real estate in more detail in later chapters.

Another form of investing is starting a business. A business can be a sole proprietorship, partnership or a corporation. You could buy into a franchise which is usually quite expensive but has an established system in place for capturing customers. Another business platform is becoming involved in a network marketing business, which offers a very low investment and with hard work, the opportunity of high earnings. Again, a later chapter goes into more detail on starting a business.

What to do with the remaining money in your PYF? You can start contributing as little as $25 a month to a mutual fund, segregated fund or ETF. It is advisable to find someone that can help you in making a choice as what to do and what investment is best for you. Do some shopping around and find a financial planner that can help you out.

There are several ways that planners are compensated, fee based, commission based (those that make commissions from the products they provide) and a hybrid of the two. It is important to clarify how they make their money before you hire them. By investing on a monthly basis, you will be using the principle of dollar cost averaging and if you buy a registered product you will also take advantage of government incentives to increase your growth, more on these later.

Remember, depending on your timing you may be looking for investment of your emergency fund as well as the remainder of the PYF. The emergency fund investment needs to be highly liquid, low risk and higher growth than PYF. The focus on the remaining funds in PYF is on growth. Liquidity is not so much an issue, as the remaining funds are invested for the long term. One item of concern is risk, which involves your comfort zone, age and time line for goals. The financial planner / advisor can help you with the selection of the right product.

Chapter Summary

There are many different places to invest your money and we touched on a few above. To begin with, stick to those which are professionally managed and use a financial planner / advisor.

Below is your action list for this chapter;
1. Shop around for a financial planner or advisor to help you with your first investments.
2. Contact the author, through the appendix information for your planner needs.
3. Begin researching information on Mutual Funds, Segregated Funds and ETFs.

We will be going into more detail on the investment choices mentioned above in later chapters, but as you can see there is much to learn before we can feel good about investing on our own. Keeping that in mind, we will be switching gears for the time being and concentrate on obtaining knowledge.

Chapter Eight – Self-Improvement

We have already looked at turning negative events (failures) into positive ones by learning as much as possible from them. This is a form of self improvement or education, learning from experiences. Michael Jordan, former professional basketball player, says, "I've failed over and over again in my life and that is why I succeed." Another form of learning comes from reading books, magazines, newspapers and even the internet. Three additional forms come from formal education, subject research and television. Life itself is a continuous learning process and if you want to be successful and achieve the goals you have set, you will have to keep on learning.

Experience, whether it is past or present, will enable you to set the future. It can include both, negative and positive events, these events should be dissected, to find out how they worked or why they did not. Present experience should be evaluated the same way by figuring out what is working and what is not. Common sense dictates that we attempt to repeat those events that were successful and avoid those that were not. By dissecting and analyzing both types of events, you may find that the negative one may be reusable with modifications or the positive one may become even better with minor changes.

The more you read the more knowledge you will amass. This is very true, but you only have so much time to absorb the information in those readings. If you were to spend all your time reading, you would spend very little time trying to achieve your goal. Therefore, you have to focus your reading towards your goal and try to set specific guidelines of content and time. Spend one hour of every single day towards reading non-fiction works geared towards your goals. There is a plethora of reading material out there and it does not mean that everything you have to read is specifically about your particular goals. Other topics to include should be on finance, accounting, sales, marketing, real estate and the list goes on.

Start with this book and then go to the bookstore, library or the Internet to get the material you need. Don't think that you can read this book and it is all you will ever need to reach your goals. Consider this book as your information introduction and try to add to your knowledge base and develop your style. So right now, select exactly when every day you are going to read and stick to it. After one year, you will have 365 hours of knowledge to put in your tool belt for your use. Chapter 47of this book contains a list of suggested book titles and media programs to peruse.

Formal education is the enrollment in a program and following is a list of examples (these are not in any priority order):

1. High School
2. College
3. University
4. Online courses
5. Correspondence courses
6. Continuing education (night school)
7. Seminars
8. Distance learning
9. Others

The list above shows you the different formats you can use. One item to keep in the back of your mind, it is relatively unimportant what piece of paper you earn from these programs, but what knowledge you take out of them that counts. The late Jim Rohn (Author and Motivational Speaker) said, "Formal education will make you a living; self-education will make you a fortune."

Funny, you mention the word "research" and shudders go down most peoples' spines. This educational format can be very motivational and exciting. Pick anyone you like, who you know to be successful and find out all you can about them. Just like you analyze your experiences, analyze their lives and see where they went right and where they went wrong. Within your research, you will discover the good, the bad and the ugly. Their successes will motivate you and the right person can be used as a silent mentor, think of what they would do in your situation. Research also includes looking into those investments that fall in line with your goals.

Television can also provide an education. **Caution though, you have to be very selective of what you are watching and the time you are spending doing it.** An incredible amount of television programs exist that are geared towards real estate, investment, history etc. Let's say you are very real estate oriented, there are shows on home improvement, preparing a house for sale, flipping properties, landscaping just to name a few. Should you decide to watch some television programming, you might surprise yourself with the information you gain. Try it but restrict your time watching to a maximum of 5 hours per week.

One of the most efficient ways of learning is enrolling in A.U., Automobile University. What is Automobile University? We spend a lot of time in our vehicles or riding the bus, so why not listen to self improvement programs instead of music, news or sports. You can learn a second language, learn how to become rich, listen to a narrated book, listen to motivational speakers etc. There is again a plethora of learning opportunities for you on many different forms of media, take advantage of the commuting time. Instead of building up stress because of traffic delays, you can now embrace them as more time for study.

Chapter Summary

This chapter looked at the different forms of self improvement. Without this key to wealth, you will not be able to achieve your desires. You will have to work smart and budget your time to get the optimal results. As you become better educated, you will be able to more clearly focus on your goals.

Below is your action list for this chapter;
1. Start browsing for additional education materials such as books, CDs or programs.
2. Set aside your one hour per day reading time and begin reading (start with this book).
3. Enroll in A.U. and find information you can listen to during your commutes.
4. Check Chapter 47 for a suggested book list and media list to choose from.
5. If you do not have the money to buy books and CDs, get a library card and get the materials from there.
6. Predetermine what you are going to watch on television and don't go over the 5 hours per week.

This action list made up for the smaller one on the previous chapter. Try to get this action list done before moving on to the next chapter.

Chapter Nine – Mentors

We briefly discussed silent mentors in the latter portion of the last chapter. What is a mentor? A mentor is someone who provides guidance directly or indirectly. We try to emulate this person in order to repeat their success for ourselves. Brian Tracy (Author and Speaker) says, "If you could find out what the most successful people did in any area and then you did the same thing over and over, you'd eventually get the same result they do." Mentoring is not hero worship, it entails using their experiences to help propel you on your path. A mentor can be someone who knows you or that you have access to. A mentor can also be someone you have never met, yet there is enough information or media available to provide you the guidance you need.

Nothing is as good as the experience of one on one contact unless it is the ultimate of sitting down with a mentor who has granted you an audience and asking them questions. Having more than one mentor will provide varied insights. Your first task will be to select who your first mentor shall be. If the mentor you have chosen is local to you, it may take as little as asking them out for lunch and paying the bill to get started. It would certainly be worth the price of a lunch to get invaluable information that will hasten you closer to your goals. These mentors do not have to be rock stars, just someone who has experienced success in attaining similar goals. Try inviting them to lunch and if you are lucky enough to get them to go, make sure you go to a nice place. This will be a tough assignment but well worth the price of lunch. When you talk on the phone to this prospective mentor, smile while you are talking to them (you can hear a smile). Also keep a positive mind set and expect a positive experience.

Try using this script, *"Mr. Lautischer, thank you for taking my call. I am currently working towards buying my first rental property and I know you have had phenomenal success in this area. I was hoping to take you to lunch and ask you a few questions"*. If you get a meeting, take a note pad with you.

Some mentors, charge for providing their guidance, perhaps on an hourly basis. These mentors are a phone call away and can be accessed when you or they are out of the area. Don't forget you will not only be charged their rates, but also the long distance charges. This medium makes even the remotest mentors within your reach.

A silent mentor is one that has not and may never be in contact with you, but access to their information is easily attainable. We are talking about those who have written books, compiled audio programs or video programs. Although they may be dead or alive, their information may still be relevant to your needs. With these types of mentors, you can study their information and squeeze every drop of insight contained within. Your only restriction is ruled by your personal time constraints. This information can also be retained for future reference.

Biographies and history are another form of silent mentors. Most famous people have either written their own auto-biography or writers have done all the research and present these people's lives in biographies. Caution when reading an auto-biography, the author may be somewhat biased. Biographies are normally in chronological order and detail a person's life more than they do a certain concept. A biography on Abe Lincoln's life is an example that depicts his triumphs and learning experiences. His life story explores his failing forward persistency, as Abe rises up to become one of the greatest leaders of our time.

In the lists provided in Chapter 47, you can pick and choose from a number of people and use them as silent mentors.

Chapter Summary

Mentors are a valuable tool to provide you guidance in the pursuit of your goals. Having more than one mentor will provide various insights and information. Silent mentors are the least expensive alternative and also the easiest to get to.

Below is your action list for this chapter;

1. Think of a successful person you would like to emulate and do research on this person (silent mentor).
2. Use Chapter 47 "Books and Media Lists" to find your first silent mentor.
3. Look in your local community, to see if there is someone who was successful attaining similar goals as yours and invite them to lunch.

Positive mental attitude is what we are using when we invite that mentor to lunch and expect him to say yes. This is what we will be looking at in the next chapter.

Chapter Ten – Positive Mental Attitude

Deepak Chopra (Author and Spiritual Guru) sums up the focus of this chapter, "You must find the place inside yourself where nothing is impossible." If you wish to become a millionaire you must begin to think like one. You have to develop that "can do" mind-set and take the negative thoughts out of your head. The expulsion of negative thoughts is sometimes very difficult as we are programmed by the people around us with their negative thoughts.

A good analogy of this phenomenon is the lobster tank example. You do not require a lid on a lobster tank as long as you put more than one lobster in. Only one lobster in the tank and it will have a chance to climb out, more than one in the tank and every time one tries to climb out the others will pull it back in. How does that relate? Every time we have an idea, the people around us will provide negative comments to discourage us from acting on the idea. If we have been programmed negatively, we may even dismiss the idea by ourselves. If you want to move ahead, you will have to abandon your personal negative thoughts and ignore those provided by other people.

So step one, to gaining a positive mental attitude, is to ignore negative thoughts from others. Step two is to try to flush personal negative thoughts. Next you have to develop the "can do" mind-set by believing in yourself and overcoming your fears by taking action. Finally, you must remind yourself every day to think positively, until it becomes a part of your sub-conscious mind.

Try to avoid spending too much time reading newspapers and listening to the news. Everything on there is focused primarily on negative events. Instead, feed your brain by reading a motivational book or listening to a CD program. Or why not work out your brain and your body at the same time, by listening to a program on a portable device and go for a run or to the gym. The media lures you into negative stories much like when you pass a serious accident. People with rubber necks, looking for gore and destruction, are so distracted by their search that they cause accidents themselves. Does this mean to cut out news all together? No, as you must keep abreast of current events in order to make intelligent investment decisions. It's more like cutting out negative events as much as possible, but be aware of major headlines.

The power of a positive mental attitude goes a long way towards accomplishing your goals, in fact you require it. It will enable you to push towards your goals regardless of whether you have the resources, whether there is a depression or recession, or whether you have support or not. It allows you to overcome obstacles that will stop someone else.

The ant philosophy is quite relevant. Study ants. Ants have a positive mental attitude since they will find a way to get where they are going regardless of the obstacle. They will go around, underneath and overtop to get to their goal. This is what you have to be willing to do to get to your goal.

You must concentrate thoughts on your goals so acutely, that you must live and breathe them to achieve them. Every waking minute should be focused on getting there. This is why it is important that you set the right goals and continuously update them to reflect where you want to go. The founder of Buddhism, Gautama Siddharta stated, "What we think, we become." If you think negative thoughts, like you can't do something, you will attract that outcome. If you think that you can do something such as attain your goals then you will attract that outcome.

Chapter Summary

Using a positive mental attitude alone will not get you to your goals, but without it, you will not reach them. Stay away from those negative thoughts and influences and replace them with that "Can Do" mind-set. One more quote from W. Clement Stone (Author), "Whatever the mind of man can conceive and believe, it can achieve." If you want to attract your goals, you have to believe it is possible, work towards them and they will come.

Below is your action list for this chapter;
1. Find a strong rubber band, put on your wrist and for one month, every time a negative thought creeps into your mind, snap yourself.
2. Every day, when you wake recite this tidbit from Tom Hopkins (Author and Sales Great), "I am a winner, a contributor, and an achiever. I believe in me!"
3. Obtain an Audio program from Jim Rohn or Zig Ziglar and listen to this instead of watching, reading or listening to the news. You can also listen to this program in A.U. or while working out.

The last action will go a long way to motivate and provide you with a positive mental attitude. Listen once and it will subject you to new ideas. Listen to it over and over again and it will serve to reprogram your subconscious. The next chapter is fairly brief and describes setting up a journal.

Chapter Eleven – My Journal

Your journal is very much like a diary, but the entries that you make should be restricted to all items related to your goals. Record your progress, actions, achievements, ideas and of course goals. You are expected to write in it each and every day. The best time for this is just before you go to sleep, this way you will also reflect on the day. Keep it by your bedside, in case an idea comes to you in the middle of the night. If you wait until morning, you run the risk of forgetting the idea.

Obtain a journal at any bookstore, it is best to find a journal with blank lined pages and no other distracters in it. At the front of the book, write out your goals and why you need to achieve them. . It is important to hand write your journal. Do not use a computer based journal, as retention is enhanced by writing information out by hand and you will be pasting clippings within.

Leave at least one blank page after your goals page in case you expand or update your goals. The very next page should be used to create a vision board. What is a vision board? Tape pictures of goals into this vision board, if your goal is to obtain a million dollars, then find a picture of one million dollars and paste it in. If another goal is to donate $100,000 to a charity you are interested in, find a picture that symbolizes the charity, write $100,000 on it and paste it in.

Every night when you are ready to make entries into your journal, flip to the first page, read your goals and your why, then flip to gaze at your vision board. Now flip to the current entry page. Each entry is started by entering the date and day of the week. Leave at least two lines at the end of recording each day's events and ideas, before starting the next, just in case you remember something you forgot to record. When you have completely filled the journal, mark the date started as well as the date of the last entry on the cover and start a new one.

Once a month, read what occurred in the past month. Once a year, read what occurred in the past year. Treasure these journals as they will serve to remind you of where you have been and are going. These journals are to be held as reference books and added to your library. They may also provide you with material should you consider writing a book.

What do you write in this journal? You will only record the actions, ideas and accomplishments that are directly related to your goals. Actions will include anything you did during that day that will bring you closer to your goals. Let's say your goals include a certain standard of physical fitness and the description of your goal is to be 160 lbs. with 10% body fat. Anything involved with attaining that goal should be listed, such as bought a tennis racket, went for a run, lifted weights, played soccer, your weight that day, etc. Included in this can be the reading of any books, magazines, listening to audio programs etc. related to your goals. Things not included would be reading a fictional book, going for dinner, entertainment through T.V. or movies, etc.

Anytime you come up with an idea or something you want to do in the future, such as obtaining a certain book, list it in the journal and place a star next to it. List any accomplishments with a star as well. For example, one of your goals is to read 78 books in a two year period and today you finished reading book number 54. These stars are reserved for important notes such as the ones described above.

Chapter Summary

The purpose of a journal is to reinforce your goals and document your progress towards them. Also to capture your thoughts, so they don't disappear. This constant documentation every day will remind you of your path and will develop discipline. The reviewing of the information every month and every year will stimulate your thought processes and allow you to remember and tweak ideas.

Below is your action list for this chapter;

1. Buy a journal from the book store. Remember to keep it simple with blank, lined pages.
2. Place your goals on the first pages and vision board on the following page. Repeat this process each time you start a new journal.
3. After completing each journal, place the "to and from" dates on the front cover.

The next chapter deals with discovering where you are in relation to your financial goals. You need to have a grasp on your financial condition right now, so you can measure and see your positive progress.

Chapter Twelve – Where Am I?

In order to determine whether you are making positive progress, you must be able to somehow measure it. We use "Net Worth" to accomplish this. What is net worth? Net worth is the difference between assets and liabilities. A person can have a negative net worth when total liabilities are larger than total assets and a positive net worth when total assets are larger than total liabilities.

Assets are the things that you own such as real estate, stocks, bonds, mutual funds etc. Some authors go a step further and state that it is only an asset if it produces a return. Items such as a personal home, vehicles, jewelry etc. should not be included as assets. For your purposes, include all items you own, as more often than not the banks will use this information and not exclude these personal assets. At least be aware, that there are good assets and bad assets. Good assets produce a return or provide you with cash flow and bad assets are ones that need money for upkeep and do not provide cash flow.

Liabilities are debts that you owe, for instance, mortgages, lines of credit, car loans, etc. Believe it or not, just like assets, there is good debt and bad debt. We will be looking at this phenomenon in another chapter titled, "Good Credit, Bad Credit".

So to determine Net Worth you subtract the total of liabilities from the total of assets and the remaining amount is your net worth. It is possible to own millions of dollars of assets and also owe millions of dollars and have a very small net worth or even have a negative net worth. The suggested goal for you, is to achieve a net worth of a million dollars, this will label you as a millionaire.

Your net worth should be updated at least once a month so that progress can be measured. Instead of having to manually calculate net worth every month, invest in a computer program that will keep track of all your spending, income, assets and liabilities. There are numerous programs out there that are capable of providing your net worth at an instant. Just remember that output is only as good as input. Therefore, you have to enter information on a timely and accurate basis.

You do not require a course in accounting to operate these programs, but you will need to learn how to read financial statements to facilitate research on stocks and business. Also, you will need to understand debits and credits and basic accounting. Financial statements are to businesses what net worth is to people, they tell you of the overall financial health of the entity. Whereas, all accounting entries require a debit (positive) and a credit (negative). For instance, the following transaction, buying a property with cash and a mortgage will result in the following entries. The property would be the debit and the resulting credits would be to cash and the mortgage payable. All debits must equal all credits.

Chapter Summary

The determination of net worth is essential for three reasons, first, to find out where you are right now. Secondly, to be able to chart your progress and finally, to make sure you are headed in the right direction. You need to know basic accounting, as this will enable understanding and interpreting financial statements.

Below is your action list for this chapter;

1. Determine your Net Worth as of today (manually). Just list all you own and all you owe. Total each and subtract the liabilities from the assets.
2. Obtain a computer program that is user friendly, this will allow you to track your income, expenses and net worth easier. Remember, quality inputs for an accurate output.
3. Search and sign up for a basic accounting course, where you will learn about debits, credits and how to read financial statements.

Earlier in the chapter, we mentioned that credit can be good and bad. How is that possible? The next chapter should answer that question.

Chapter Thirteen – Good Credit, Bad Credit

When does credit become good? The following will answer this question, but first we have to define what credit is. According to the Merriam Webster's Collegiate Dictionary (tenth edition), "Credit" has several definitions but for our purpose we will use 1: c: "time given for payment for goods or services sold on trust". So the goods or services are received today on a promise that payment will take place on a future date or series of future dates.

So then what is bad credit? Bad credit is when you create an obligation to pay for consumer goods or for items that do not produce a return. Examples include buying groceries on a credit card, using a line of credit to buy a boat, obtaining a car loan to purchase a vehicle or even using a mortgage to buy the home you are living in. Some bad credit choices are almost impossible to avoid such as buying a home in which to live. The upside potential of buying a home to live is that it may appreciate in value over time and at the end of the mortgage you will still have an asset with value as opposed to renting and having nothing at the end of the lease. Even if credit is used to purchase an asset that provides a return, when the return is less than the rate of interest charged, it is considered bad credit.

Therefore, good credit is when we purchase an asset that provides a return that is greater than the cost of the credit. Let's say we buy a bond with a line of credit and the rate of interest on the line of credit is 4% but the rate of interest paid on the bond is 6%, the difference is 2% on the original amount. In Canada, in addition to the 2% we would be getting from the return, we can use the interest paid of 4% as a tax deduction, thereby in effect increasing the return on the bond. This wise use of credit puts money in your pocket. Notice in the example, we didn't use a penny of our own money. Further chapters will discuss both income tax and the use of OPM (other peoples' money).

Where most people go wrong is they obtain lines of credit to buy depreciating (as time goes forward the value decreases) assets, consumable goods or assets that require money for upkeep such as a vehicle. The interest on these purchases, are not tax deductable. You could also lose money in three different ways, interest, upkeep costs and decreasing value. You are better off to buy these purchases with money you have saved. Remember, an emergency fund is always better than a line of credit. The reason being, that the line of credit itself, becomes bad credit.

Chapter Summary

Good credit involves buying assets that provide a greater return than the cost of interest and are income tax deductable. Bad credit is when we use credit to buy depreciable assets or consumer goods most of which are not tax deductable.

Below is your action list for this chapter;
1. Use credit wisely, try to reduce your bad debt and determine if you have any good debt. Start by eliminating credit with highest interest rate (usually credit cards).
2. If you don't have a line of credit, inquire with your banking institution if you are eligible for one. If you are eligible, find out what the interest rate is.
3. Consider obtaining a line of credit and if you decide to get one, **only use it for good credit!**

Don't forget, work at reducing bad credit and be ready with that line of credit if an opportunity comes up. The next chapter talks about the best income of all, Passive Income.

Chapter Fourteen – Passive Income

One of the keys to becoming wealthy is to develop independent multiple streams of income. If any one of the streams dries up or stops for any reason, then remaining ones, being unaffected, should still come in. There are basically two types of income, active and passive income. We are limited as to how many streams of active income can be developed whereas infinite streams of passive income is possible.

Active income comes in as a result of our efforts. The most common generated active income is from employment or self-employment, but anytime we physically have to do something in order to receive income, it is labeled as "active". A well known cliché heard from many employees is, "working hard for your money" and implies that if we did not work for it, we would not receive compensation.

Passive income makes your money work for you. This income does not come from your efforts, but most commonly will come from money creating money. Examples of this include; dividends received from investment in stocks or businesses, rental income from real estate, interest earned from bonds, savings accounts, loans, etc. You do not have to work for this money, in fact you can do other things and it still comes in. This is why it is somewhat limitless or infinite. Once a stream is initiated, you can set up another and so on. Most wealthy people take advantage of this concept and completely replace active income with passive income. **One of your goals should be to strive to build up multiple streams of passive income.** Someday, you will have enough coming in to replace your active income and will have the choice whether or not to continue with your job. If you choose to continue working, your active income is just a part of the multiple streams and the choice to stop should always be available. This goes a long way to create peace of mind.

At this point, you can replace the word "income" with "cash flow" as they can be used synonymously. Essentially money received from any source is cash inflow and money paid is outflow. You can set up these multiple streams of passive cash flow within or outside your PYF account. Just remember, all cash flow produced from within must remain within, whereas cash flow created outside only requires you submit your predetermined percentage back in to the PYF.

Chapter Summary

Active cash flow is money you receive that is generated by personal efforts and passive cash flow is money you receive as a result of your money working for you. Active cash flows are limited by your time whereas passive ones are limitless. Building up multiple streams of passive cash flow is a concept used extensively by wealthy people. Money received is equal to cash inflow and money paid is equal to cash outflow.

Below is your action list for this chapter;
1. Look all the different forms of cash flow you are currently receiving and determine whether they are active or passive.
2. Add to your personal goals by determining an amount of passive cash flow you would like to generate by a certain date and your reason why. A reason why could be, "To maintain my expected lifestyle and have the time and freedom to enjoy it"
3. Another possible goal would be to replace your active cash flow with passive cash flow by a certain date.
4. Strive to add multiple streams of passive cash flow to your financial picture.

Growth is the percentage that an investment increases by. It includes passive cash flow received, as well earnings left in an investment. Growth is magnified through the use of compound interest. Compound interest, in turn, is magnified by two variables that will be discussed in the next chapter.

Chapter Fifteen – Compound Interest

What would you rather have $1,000,000 or a penny compounded daily at 100% interest for a month? The table below shows the calculation;

Day	Interest	Total	Day	Interest	Total
1	.01	.02	17	655.36	1310.72
2	.02	.04	18	1310.72	2621.44
3	.04	.08	19	2621.44	5242.88
4	.08	.16	20	5242.88	10485.76
5	.16	.32	21	10485.76	20971.52
6	.32	.64	22	20971.52	41943.04
7	.64	1.28	23	41943.04	83886.08
8	1.28	2.56	24	83886.08	167772.16
9	2.56	5.12	25	167772.16	335544.32
10	5.12	10.24	26	335544.32	671088.64
11	10.24	20.48	27	671088.64	1342177.28
12	20.48	40.96	28	1342177.28	2684354.56
13	40.96	81.92	29	2684354.56	5368709.12
14	81.92	163.84	30	5368709.12	10737418.24
15	163.84	327.68	31	10737418.24	21474836.48
16	327.68	655.36			

A penny compounded daily at 100% after 31 days equals $21,474,836.48. This shows the power of compound interest. The two variables that have the greatest effect on compounding is time and interest rate.

Compounding occurs when the interest earned is not taken in payment but left in the investment. Every time you achieve growth it is put back into the original pot and interest is not only made on the principal (amount invested) but also on the interest put back in. Each time the interest is put back in, a new principal starting point occurs and this continual expansion of a new starting point multiplies itself over time.

The "Rule of 72"shows you the amazing effect of compounding and the importance of obtaining a better rate. The rule states that your money will approximately DOUBLE at a point in time determined by dividing 72 by the interest rate you earn. Using this simple formula, you can calculate the time it takes to double your money at certain rates. For instance, 8% annual rate compounded annually will take 72 / 8 = **9 years to double**, 10% annual rate compounded annually will take 72 / 10 = **7.2 years**, 12% annual rate compounded annually will take 72 / 12 = **6 years**, etc. By compounding monthly or daily you will further reduce the time required to double.

Compounding has a dramatic effect on your investments and can have an equally catastrophic effect on your cash flow, if it is in the form of a debt. A good example of this is credit card debt where only the minimum payment is made each month.

Even when you hold an investment that pays out the interest or growth every month, you can still take advantage of compounding by placing that growth into another account that pays interest. A good example is any money paid out from any investment held in your PYF, is put back in the fund to earn further growth. Consider the growth as your initial investment's children and those children having children and so on.

Chapter Summary

Compound interest can have remarkable effect on your investments and is affected by time and growth rate. Equally devastating is the effect that compound interest has on your debts. To calculate how long it will approximately take your investments to double, use the "Rule of 72", divide 72 by the interest rate.

Below is your action list for this chapter;
1. Look at your credit card debt once again and determine which has the highest rate of interest and work at reducing those first.
2. Research your bank accounts that pay interest. Find out when they pay

that interest and what percentage is paid. Then calculate how long it will take to double your investment using the rule of 72. You will be surprised by the length of the doubling period and the benefit of getting the best possible rate.

To this point, you have not taken into account what effect income taxes have on our investments. In the next chapter, we will briefly discuss Income Tax implications and some strategies to minimize taxes.

Chapter Sixteen – Income Tax

Any growth you make from any investments will result in income taxes owing. There are some exceptions that you will be exposed to later. Any time you make money from investments the Canada Revenue Agency expects that you will pay income taxes. With this in mind, it is wise to plan to minimize taxes owing. You must account for taxes in determining the growth rate of investments. Not every type of growth is equally taxed.

In descending order; interest income is taxed at the fullest extent meaning any income will be taxed at your top marginal tax rate, most dividend income qualifies for a dividend tax credit and results in a lower tax rate, capital gains accrues the lowest form of taxation and only 50% of the gain is taxable. Again, a quick definition of each type of income is in order.

Interest Income is growth that results from savings accounts, loans, bonds etc. Dividends are monies paid out by corporations to their shareholders from common stock, preferred shares, private companies etc. It is usually a distribution of profits that have already been taxed to the corporation. Capital gains and losses usually results from the sale of assets at a higher or lower rate than they were purchased for and examples include sale of stocks, bonds, real estate, etc.

In Canada, taxes are calculated on a graduated system. Each bracket of income is taxed at a higher rate as the level of income rises. Marginal tax rate is the top bracket that you fall into for calculation of taxes. This means that each additional dollar income you make will be subjected to this top rate. It is important to know this rate, as this will also determine the amount deductions will save you in taxes.

As mentioned in previous chapters, when you borrow money to make business income, most of the time any interest you pay is tax deductable. There are rules governing this deduction but it is well worth looking into. This deduction actually adds to the growth rate of the investment. For example, you borrow $1000 at the interest rate of 5% and you use the $1000 to buy a bond that pays interest of 6%, you will make 1% of 1000 ($10). In addition, you will also be able to claim an income tax deduction of $50 (at a marginal tax rate of 36% of $50 equals $18 or another 1.8%) making a total cash flow of $28 or 2.8% on 1000. In this example, you have not used your own money, so the return on investment is infinite.

There are certain investments that are registered with the government that either defer income tax or completely absolve paying any taxes. Examples of these include Registered Retirement Savings Plans (RRSP) and Tax Free Savings Accounts (TFSA). These programs will be detailed in future chapters.

A word of caution, you are trying to minimize your taxes payable and not trying to evade taxes, which is illegal. It is advisable that anytime you are considering minimizing taxes that you obtain professional help and advice. Have your yearly taxes prepared by professionals, as they will provide you with peace of mind and will normally correspond with government on any problems encountered.

Chapter Summary

Interest income is taxed at the highest rate, dividend income usually qualifies for a dividend tax credit and only 50% of capital gains are taxable. Interest costs are normally deductable when borrowing funds for the purpose of investment. Some registered products can defer taxes and some even excuse the payment of taxes. Use professionals for tax planning and preparation.

Below is your action list for this chapter;
1. Do some research and find out exactly under what circumstances you can borrow money to make investments and be able to deduct the interest cost. Start with the internet.
2. Start looking around for a firm to prepare your taxes. Make sure they

are willing to correspond with the government on your behalf.

3. Determine what your marginal tax rate is. This can be achieved by perusing your last tax return.

One more way to minimize your annual income tax bill is discussed in the next chapter.

Chapter Seventeen – Home Office

Another excellent way to minimize taxes is to take advantage of using a home office for business purposes. The Canada Revenue Agency allows the deduction of any reasonable current expense you paid or will have to pay to earn business income including business use of home expenses. To be eligible the space designated must be your principal place of business or you use the space only to earn your business income, and you use it on a regular and ongoing basis to meet your clients, customers, or patients.

Deductions include heating, home insurance, electricity, property taxes, mortgage interest, and Capital Cost Allowance (CCA). Let's say you have designated a room specifically for business purposes, in order to calculate the portion of deductable expenses you must first obtain the square footage of the room and the total house. Divide the room space by total house and multiply the total expense to determine the business use allocation. For example, you have designated the den, which is 250 square feet and the total house is 1500 square feet. The total electricity charge for the entire year was $1000 and you used the home office the entire year strictly for business purposes. The calculation then is 250/1500 X $1000 = $166.67 and this amount can be used as a deduction for electricity for the home office for the year.

Calculations will have to be adjusted if the space was used for both business and personal living. Also, the use of CCA deduction on the work space can have repercussions when selling the home later. It is advised that you consider not using CCA in determining deductions. You are limited to the amount allowed for home office expenses as it cannot be more than the net income.

The details of this deduction can be found on the Canada Revenue Agency website at http://www.cra-arc.gc.ca and reference Line 9945. There are numerous other deductions and strategies to reduce income taxes. The information on these can be provided by tax lawyers, accountants, tax preparers and financial planners.

Chapter Summary

Use of a home office to earn business income, can provide a deduction on your income taxes. The calculation to determine the amount of deduction is simply, room square footage divided by total footage multiplied by the total expense. Details can be found at the CRA website.

Below is your action list for this chapter;
1. Peruse the CRA website and read the information on home office expenses and see if this deduction applies to you.

2. Consult with a professional on more deductions available and refer to people listed in chapter 23.

Now that we have some basics down, the next chapter on Tax Free Savings Accounts will demonstrate how you can become a millionaire with just this one program.

Chapter Eighteen – TFSA (Million Dollar Idea)

The Tax Free Savings Account or TFSA was created by the Government of Canada to encourage Canadians to save money. This registered account allows the growth of the investment to accrue tax free. This means that any money you invest in the account cannot be used as a tax deduction but any growth as a result of the account, grows tax free. As you will see later, the government has created a means for you to become a millionaire.

Below is a point form description of the TFSA;

- Canadian Residents, over the age of 18, can contribute up to a maximum of $5000 per year
- Investment income earned is tax free
- Unused contributions each year can be carried forward for future years, the program started in 2009 and if you have made no contributions thus far, in 2013 you can contribute $25,000
- All withdrawals are tax free and any of these can be paid back but to avoid penalties they should be paid back in the year following the year they were withdrawn
- Contrary to the name, "Savings Account", investments can vary widely and can include stocks,

mutual funds, segregated funds, bonds, etc.

So how can you make a million dollars? Using discipline, compound interest, time and research, you can formulate a plan to become a millionaire. Here is the theory part, if we start at the age of 18, invest the allowable TFSA maximum of $5000 per year, obtain a 10% growth rate (compounded annually), at the end of 31 years we will have $954,119 in that account. By changing some of the variables such as contributing the maximum ($416.66) every month instead of annually or obtaining a better growth rate or compounding monthly will increase the end result.

Realizing of course that we might not have the luxury of starting at 18, we again can change variables such as having two people contribute at the same time. An example includes, both your significant other and you make the maximum contributions. In this case at the end of 25 years, you each will have about $515,736. The figures above were calculated using the Government of Canada TFSA website calculator and amounts may vary depending on programs and variables used. The point is, at the end of 31 years you could have approximately a million dollars tax free to spend as you like. This is in addition to any pensions being collected, other investments or other streams of income.

A big question you may have is where do you get an investment that pays 10%? Well, this is where the research comes in. At the time of this writing, bank rates are at an all time low and bank savings accounts are paying next to nothing. There are investments currently out there that provide 10% or more and may involve more risk. You will have to take action and do some research to discover those higher growth products.

Chapter Summary

The Tax Free Savings Account allows you to invest up to $5000 per year and accrue growth tax free. The combination of investing in the TFSA, time, compounding, research and discipline provides us with an investment vehicle that can make you a millionaire. A great perk of the TFSA is that withdrawals from the plan are tax free. Imagine having built up one million dollars in this account and still getting 10% growth, you could pull out $100,000 a year tax free and never touch the principle amount.

Below is your action list for this chapter;
1. It is never too late, start a TFSA as soon as possible.
2. Start researching where you can get the rates you desire for this account. We suggest, with limited knowledge in investing, you start by looking at segregated funds, mutual funds or ETF's as they have professional

managers and can provide higher rates of growth.

3. Schedule an appointment with an investment advisor or planner and discuss what they have to offer or access to in the way of TFSAs.

4. Another alternative is to contact the author using the appendix at the back of the book.

You may consider using TFSA accounts for the investment portion of your emergency fund. This provides easy access, there are no penalties to withdraw from it and you can replace your withdrawals at a future date. Tax Free Savings Accounts are just one of the strategies to become wealthy, in this next chapter we will look at another registered account that provides tremendous growth potential, the Registered Retirement Savings Plan.

Chapter Nineteen – RRSP

Registered Retirement Savings Plans or as they are more commonly known, RRSPs, are another registered plan offered by the government. The purpose of this plan is to assist Canadians to prepare for retirement. It acts as a supplement to other forms of retirement plans such as Canada Pension Plan (CPP) and Old Age Security (OAS). It is entirely voluntary and the allowable contributions are based on the previous year's taxable earnings.

RRSPs provide a tax deduction for the amount contributed and allow tax free growth while within the plan. Any money taken out of the plan is taxable in the year received and you are not able to re-contribute those amounts in the future. Let's say you have $25,000 in an RRSP account and during the year you take out $5000, you will be taxed on that $5000 as regular income and you cannot replace the $5000 in future years. Any unused contributions are eligible for carry forward to future years. For example let's say in 2012, your carry forward of unused contributions is $50,000 and in 2013 you are allowed the maximum of $23,500 contribution and did not use it. The current contribution of $23,500 will now be added to your carry forward of $50,000 and in 2014 you will be allowed to use $73,500 as well as the current contribution.

RRSPs provide the opportunity for tremendous growth, as not only will you reap the benefit of growth from investments in the plan but each contribution provides a refund of tax and the proper use of the refund will accelerate your investment program. The refund should be used for funding next year's contribution to an RRSP or for investment in a TFSA or at the very least a percentage of the refund goes back to your PYF fund. Although it is common practice to borrow money to contribute to RRSPs and TFSAs, we advise not to, as any interest paid for the purpose of funding these is not tax deductable.

Although RRSPs only defer taxes owing, this becomes another way to make a million dollars. The growth accumulates tax free just like TFSAs. The contribution limits can be higher than the TFSAs and you're receiving sizable refunds for further investment. For these two reasons, you should be able to shorten the time span to get to a million dollars. Pretty well most of the investments allowed for TFSAs are also allowed for RRSPs, some exceptions may apply.

If you maximize contributions in RRSPs and TFSAs and get your significant other involved you will significantly shorten the time it takes to achieve a million dollar goal. Keeping this in mind, you should make use of both of these investments to put your financial house in order.

In chronological order, obtain a will, buy term life insurance if needed, establish an emergency fund, maximize your RRSP contributions and use tax refunds provided to maximize your TFSA. Any money left over after this will be used for further investments discussed in future chapters.

Chapter Summary

Registered Retirement Savings Plans provide the opportunity to defer taxes and provide a supplement for you during retirement. RRSPs are yet another easy way to reaching a million dollar goal. Use your refund to inject into further investments to accelerate your plan and don't squander it on consumable goods.

Below is your action list for this chapter;
1. Determine what your unused RRSP contribution is at. This can be found on your notice of assessment from the previous year's income taxes.
2. Determine your current year contribution limit. This can also be found on the same notice.
3. Research on your own or enlist a financial advisor / planner to locate investments that fit within your guidelines for investment in RRSPs or TFSAs.

4. Once again for help with this, you can contact the author with the information found in the appendix. The next chapter will focus on a very feasible and efficient way of purchasing investments.

Chapter Twenty – Dollar Cost Averaging

Dollar cost averaging is an excellent way of investing in mutual funds, segregated funds, ETFs and stocks. Most people try to time lump sum purchases and make the fatal mistake of buying high and selling low. It is very difficult, if not impossible, to time the market. Dollar cost averaging takes out the guesswork and involves purchasing an investment on a regular basis (usually monthly) with a specific amount of money. This allows you to buy fewer units when the cost is high and more units when the cost is low. Over time this will allow you to buy the investment at a lower cost assuming markets always increase.

Look at any chart detailing the Canadian stock market over the past fifty years and you will discover that the stock prices have always increased. Of course there will be ups and downs, fluctuations caused by differing economies, but overall the markets are always rising. Using dollar cost averaging, buy and hold philosophy and picking solid investments will serve to take the guess work out of when to buy.

Let's look at an example and say you have two choices, to buy 500 XYZ Stock at $10.00 today for $5,000 or spend $1000 each month for 5 months. The following are the XYZ prices starting today and each month's anniversary date for 5 months. Today = $10, month 2 = $9, month 3 = $11, month 4 = $8, month 5 = $10, month 6 = $12. At the end of month 6, your lump sum purchase went from $5,000 to $6,000 and the dollar cost averaging purchase went from $5,000 (100+111.11+90.91+125+100=527.02) 527 X $12 = $6324.00. This example assumes we have price fluctuations.

DATE	$ XYZ	# Shrs.	$	TOT. $
today	$10	100	$1000	$1000
Mo. 2	$9	111.1	$1000	$1899
Mo. 3	$11	90.9	$1000	$3322
Mo. 4	$8	125	$1000	$3416
Mo. 5	$10	100	$1000	$5270
Mo. 6	$12	527	D.C.A.	$6324
Mo. 6	$12	500	LUMP	$6000

You may not have the capital to buy an investment with a lump sum or you may see the advantage that dollar cost averaging provides. Dollar cost averaging allows you to participate right now and uses compounding more efficiently. This will in turn, provide a lower cost and accelerate your growth.

An important point to consider when using dollar cost averaging is whether there is a higher commission or sales charge than buying with a lump sum. This may depend also on when the sales charge is administered. Some investments will not have a sales charge, some will have a front load charge (meaning it is paid at initial purchase) and some will have a deferred declining sales charge (paid at time of withdrawal that decreases over time). If the buy and hold strategy is used, then a deferred declining sales charge is unimportant, as at some point the sales charge is eliminated entirely.

Chapter Summary

Dollar cost averaging is advantageous as it allows immediate participation, makes use of compounding and over time, buys the investment at the lowest possible price. Combine the buy and hold strategy and choose solid investments to maximize growth. Remember to consider what the sales charges are and their effect on the growth of your investment.

Below is your action list for this chapter;
1. Practice calculating what it would cost for a lump sum investment and use of dollar cost averaging by selecting 5 different mutual funds. Locate the historical costs and figure out how many units a $12,000 investment one year ago would get and then calculate investing $1,000 per month from that date. You need to figure out how many units a month you could purchase and total the number of units. Compare the funds

and see if one way obtains more units.
2. Evaluate your own investments and consider switching to dollar cost averaging.
3. Consider contributing on a monthly basis to purchase an investment through a TFSA or RRSP. Ask a financial advisor or planner for assistance in selecting the right investment for you until you gain the expertise to do it yourself.

Every investment carries a level of uncertainty in its performance and because we are all unique, we all have different tolerance levels of this uncertainty. This is the subject of the next chapter.

Chapter Twenty One – Risk and Tolerance

Two main variables determine the amount of risk involved in any investment and they are liquidity and safety of capital. Generally, as we get older (nearer to retirement) and/or we require the use of our investments to supplement our income, we need our investments to become more liquid and safer. When we are younger, we can afford to take more chances and we can trade the level of risk for higher growth.

Liquidity is the fast transformation from investment to cash. Examples of extremely liquid investments include savings accounts, bonds, publicly traded stocks etc. Some will argue that stocks are not liquid, but because stocks are traded on a secondary market, stock exchanges, they are convertible to cash very quickly. Semi-liquidity is the ability to convert to cash within one month. Other examples of less liquid investments include term deposits or guaranteed investment certificates (GICs) that take longer than a month to cash.

At the other end of the spectrum, are non-liquid investments such as real estate, which may take months to years to convert. Remember, you should have already considered liquid to semi- liquid investments for your emergency fund. One way to reduce the need for liquidity in the rest of your regular investments is to increase your emergency fund to cover one year's income.

Safety of capital refers to those investments that may provide less growth but tend to hold their value. Examples can include savings accounts, Guaranteed Investment Certificates (GICs), term deposits, most bonds etc. Some investments that are tangible assets such as real estate, collectables etc. are safer but do provide challenges such as finding a buyer upon disposal.

You can use your age to determine an approximate guideline for the amount of safety and liquidity required. For example, if you are 45 years of age add 15 to your age to come up the percentage of conservative investments, then 60% of your investments should be in safer and more liquid products and the remaining 40% in growth and more risk. At 65 years of age, you should have approximately 80% in conservative investments and 20% in more aggressive investments. Note, these are just rough guidelines and depending on your personal tolerance, these figures should be adjusted.

Your personal tolerance levels are determined by your own peace of mind. Are you willing to risk more for an aggressive portfolio and be able to sleep at night or do you need to have less risk, so you are not constantly thinking about your investments?

There are other ways to reduce risk in addition to the ones discussed above.

Diversifying your investment portfolio between different investments helps to manage risk. When we speak of diversity we mean between stocks, bonds, real estate, mutual funds, cash, and near cash accounts, etc. You can diversify even deeper by spreading your funds within each of those different investments. An example includes acquiring stocks in a silver mining company, a major bank, a telecommunications company and a clothing company.

Another way to minimize risk includes shopping around, as there are many investments to choose from. Do extensive research before purchasing. For stock purchases, research includes using both fundamental and technical analysis techniques (more on these in a later chapter).

Chapter Summary

Risk includes both safety of capital and liquidity. Determining your mix of investments (portfolio) will depend on your age and your tolerance level. Your portfolio includes all investments including the emergency fund. Any investments held in the emergency fund should be at least semi-liquid and safe. Risk can be reduced through diversity and research. Diversity is not only achieved by investment in different types of groups but also within each group. Knowledge decreases risk, so continue attending Automobile University and be an aggressive reader.

Below is your action list for this chapter;
1. Label each investment in your current investment portfolio to determine which is safer and liquid and which are less safe and not so liquid.
2. What is your current mix? (Percentage)
3. Do you worry about your investments excessively? What is your tolerance level? Can you cope with more aggressive investments or would you like to reduce your stress?
4. Using your age and tolerance level, determine what your investment mix should be. Begin moving towards the ideal percentage for you.

The next chapter looks at a technique that is used by practically all wealthy people. It is referred to as "OPM" and can dramatically increase your growth rate on investments.

Chapter Twenty Two – OPM

Imagine getting 100%, 200% or even infinite growth on your investment. This is possible when you use OPM (Other Peoples' Money or Leverage). OPM can include loans, lines of credit, investor money or whenever funds being used are not your own. An example might best demonstrate how huge the returns can be. Let's say you purchase 1000 shares of XYZ Company for $10 a share with $8000 from a line of credit and $2000 of your own money. One month later we sell the 1000 shares for $12 for a $2000 gain. This gain translates to 100% (1200% per annum) growth on your investment. You invested $2000 of your own money and now have $4000 after the borrowed $8000 is paid. If we borrowed the full amount then our growth is infinite.

When you use OPM, you are leveraging your investments. A word of caution, when using OPM you also will magnify any losses. In our last example, if instead we sold the shares for $8 we would lose 100% of our investment. A common form of leveraging with the purchase of stocks is the use of a margin account. A margin account is where the brokerage firm will lend up to 50% of the value of the stocks to purchase the same. When the price falls below the purchase price, the investor is required to deposit funds to offset losses, otherwise the account may be subject to a margin call. A margin call is when the brokerage will sell off shares held to satisfy the margin requirement. Leveraging is not restricted to purchasing stocks and can be used in the purchase of any investments. In real estate, leverage is commonly called a mortgage.

OPM usually involves costs of borrowing money, known as interest. As discussed in previous chapters, the cost of borrowing money for business and investment purposes is normally tax deductable. One of the exceptions to this rule is the purchase of government registered products such as RRSPs and TFSAs. Be careful when using OPM, as it is easy to overextend yourself, make sure you can handle the interest costs and payments required. Start by using smaller amounts and carefully analyze the benefits as well as the hazards associated with use of OPM.

Chapter Summary

The use of OPM is advantageous because it magnifies the return on the money you invest, the cost of borrowing is usually tax deductable and leveraging allows you to take part in investments that you normally couldn't. Common forms of leveraging include lines of credit, margin accounts and mortgages. Remember, that the same concept that magnifies your growth can also magnify your losses. OPM can be used for TFSA and RRSP purposes, but the interest paid is not tax deductable.

Below is your action list for this chapter;

1. Determine how much OPM you are using and express it as a percentage of the investments owned. Only include credit used for the purchase of investments, this excludes mortgages on your personal homes.
2. When starting out keep the percentage below 25%, as you gain experience and confidence you can increase your OPM percentage. Stay within your comfort range.
3. If you have not already obtained a line of credit, get one now and only use it for investment purposes.

The next chapter is also a concept that the rich use and provides them to access information and services that normally one person cannot provide.

Chapter Twenty Three – Build a Team

Being a self-made millionaire is somewhat a fallacy, you cannot do it on your own. You will have to put together a team to help you reach your goals. Wealthy people surround themselves with professionals that are good at what they do. The motive is to deal with those items where they lack the skills, knowledge or to free up time for other more important functions. The affluent also maintain an inner, like-minded, personal group of two or more. Napoleon Hill and others have labeled these people as a "mastermind" group.

When starting out, your professional group should consist of an accountant / tax advisor, banker, lawyer, real estate agent and financial planner / advisor. We will add to this group when the need arises. The process is generally the same with all the professionals you seek out. You must go and meet with these professionals in person. In some cases this initial meeting may cost. The purpose of the meeting is for you to introduce yourself, conduct an interview of the person you have picked out, state what services you are looking for and determine their rates. You should be able to keep this meeting to 15 minutes in length.

Mentioned previously, select a tax preparer (make sure it is a senior tax professional) that can prepare your taxes and serve as a tax advisor. In the action list in the chapter entitled, "Where Am I", you were asked to take an accounting course and use a simple bookkeeping program. Both the tax preparer and the bookkeeping program will do in the interim. When things become too complex or you are spending too much time bookkeeping, find an accountant, with a professional designation, who specializes in taxes. Conduct an initial meeting referred to above. Start now by keeping your ear to the ground for any possible candidates.

When selecting a banker, go to 2-3 banks, including the one you deal with now. Ask to speak to a loans specialist, explain that you are shopping around for lending institutions and looking for the one that works the best for you. Tell them that you intend on borrowing money for the purpose of investing and that you will be looking for lines of credit, mortgages and regular loans. To protect yourself, as well as the bank, tell them that any loans will be secured by using the investments as collateral. When selecting which bank to use it is important to select the one you feel most comfortable with or in other words the individual that you developed the best rapport with. Once established, visit this person once a month to keep in touch and let them know what you are doing. Most of the time, if you set up any kind of lending arrangements, you are required to set up an account. Make sure that you select the account with the least expensive bank charges. At some banks, if you maintain a minimum balance they will waive service charges. Interest rates are sometimes insignificant, as you can go to the bank with proof of what the other bank is offering and they will usually match or beat that rate. So are rates negotiable? The answer to that is yes, most banks are flexible with rates. You have to ask, you don't have to accept what the posted rate is. Remember the bible quote, "Ask and you shall receive!" As you do more business with this bank, ask to be introduced to the branch manager and extend your monthly visits with them as well.

Lawyers tend to specialize in certain areas of law. The lawyer you are looking for is one that specializes in real estate and contract law. Although, it may be premature, select one with those specializations and set up a meeting with them. You are only sitting down with one lawyer, so it is advisable to do your research ahead of time, as each meeting may cost you money. Lawyers almost always charge out based on time. Your first 15 minute meeting with the lawyer should include you introducing yourself, stating your intentions and inquiring about the rates and costs involved in buying or selling real estate. The following is an example, "Hello Mr. Mason, my name is *Your Name*. I intend on investing in Real Estate and I wish to inquire about what legal costs would be incurred in buying as well as selling. Are the rates different for commercial or residential properties? How about the cost of putting together a mortgage contract? What is your standard hourly rate? Thank you very much for your time." Make sure you take notes during the meeting and that you obtain a card with phone numbers, fax, address and email details.

Real Estate agents can specialize as well, so when searching one out determine whether or not they have in fact, owned investment property and that they have conducted commercial property deals. By phoning your local real estate office you should be able to quiz reception as to who in the office may fit the bill. Again sit down with the candidates and go with the one you feel most comfortable with. Make sure they know that at this time you are shopping around for an agent you feel most comfortable with. Take their card and tell them you will be in touch. When you are ready to invest in real estate, call them up and explain what you are looking for.

While looking for a real estate agent, enquire whether the firm provides property management services for future consideration. It is advisable to find a property manager that does property management as their only job. Unfortunately, some areas require that property managers have a real estate license. This can be both a benefit and a detriment, as it may create a conflict of interest.

Financial advisors and planners were mentioned in previous chapters and there is definitely a difference between the two. A financial advisor normally works for a particular company selling the company's product and receives compensation in the form of commissions from products sold. Whereas the financial planner has had some form of formal education and can provide you with a map or a guide for your financial plans. Financial planners can be fee based and/or receive commissions on products sold. Fee based planners charge for their services in a number of different ways but most commonly on an hourly basis. Financial planners can also obtain professional certification as a Certified Financial Planner (CFP). Seek out a financial planner and again interview them for the purpose of determining who to use. As long as you are not seeking financial planning or advice, they should provide a 15 minute interview free of charge. During your interview of the planner, ask what formal training they have received and their experience. When dealing with a financial advisor know that they are representing the company they are working for and that they will be able to provide you with limited advice and products.

The inner circle or mastermind group is 2 or more individuals that share a common goal or are like-minded. They help each other grow by providing ideas and advice to each other. Your inner circle could consist of just you and your spouse or common-law, family member, friend or someone that shares your goals. This could be a group of achievement minded people that meet once a month for lunch or breakfast to share ideas and solve each other's problems. By doing this, you make use of experiences and solutions encountered by others in similar situations.

These relationships with professionals and the creation of your inner circle will not happen overnight. This is why this chapter is entitled, "Build a Team". It will take time but the reward is worth the effort. Used properly, a team and a mastermind group will fast forward you to achieving your financial goals.

Chapter Summary

To reach your financial goals, you will have to build a team of professionals and develop an inner circle. There are no self-made millionaires, as they rely on help from others to get them where they're going. It may cost you to get your team together but it is true that you get what you pay for. Not only will it cost you money, but also time and effort.

Below is your action list for this chapter;
1. Start building your team of professionals. You may have already started, now try to complete the team with the ones listed above.
2. Consider at least one other person to start the development of your inner circle. Discuss your ideas with this person and make sure that they are

interested in doing the same. Continually update your inner circle by bringing others in and if needed, weeding others out.

The next chapter focuses on the type of people that you cannot afford to have in your inner circle or even associate with.

Chapter Twenty Four – Other's Negative Attitudes

As discussed in Chapter 10, it is essential that you have a positive mental attitude in order to be able to reach your goals. It would be great, if everyone else you associate with would have one too. We can choose our friends but not our family. In most cases, it is our family or relatives that have preconceived notions of what we can and cannot do.

Remember the story of the lobster tank? Negative people will try to pull you back down to their level. Often times when we tell others what we are doing they'll tell us; you can't do that, if that was possible someone else would have done it already, you don't have the money for that, etc.

Yes, unfortunately many times it will be your own family that shoots these negative ideas at you. There are three ways in which you can handle these ideas. First of all, you could accept what they say and hide your head in the ground like an ostrich. Secondly, you could completely ignore anything that they said and face the repercussions in your family life. Finally, you could pleasantly tell them that you see their point, but you are going to try anyway. By using the last alternative, you will channel their negativity and make it a challenge. Don't tell them you are going to use their negative thoughts to prove them wrong.

When you use this line of thought, it can sometimes push you even harder towards your goals.

An example from my past really fits here. It occurred when I was going through the application process to become a peace officer. I was working for another company and word spread that I had applied to become a peace officer. One of the managers approached me and stated that I should not even bother going through the process. He explained that his son had applied and most assuredly would get the position before I did. His reasoning was that his son attended a law enforcement college and was a much better suited candidate than I was for the job. This infuriated me and instead of lashing out, I used a combination of two of the alternatives. I ignored his comments and I used them to motivate my pursuit of the job. I transformed my anger to a burning desire, only known to myself, to get the position no matter what. The result was that out of about 1200 applicants, 26 individuals were selected for the class. I was one of them and his son was not. I held my own private celebration and never mentioned my victory to that manager. I am sure he found out regardless. Incidentally, his son did make it to another form of law enforcement within University security, showing the power of education.

So contrary to popular belief, you can use negativity in a constructive manner, but you are better to avoid it as much as possible.

It is like a disease, if you are around it too much it will actually take hold of your mind. Once it takes hold, it will destroy your plans and you'll use it to reason why you did not achieve your goals. It would be like the ant philosophy gone wrong, instead of finding a way to your goal you go back to the ant hill and never venture out again.

Chapter Summary

As much as possible, avoid negative people and where this is not possible, use their negativity as a motivator or a challenge to catapult you to your goals. Remember the ant philosophy. Your inner circle should not have any negative thinking people. Make sure you have a celebration each time you or anyone in your inner circle reaches a goal. This will reinforce positive action and outcomes.

Below is your action list for this chapter;
1. Go through your list of friends and see who is negative and who is positive. Spend more time with those positive people and less to no time with the negative people.
2. When you come across negativity, use it as a challenge to reach your goals.
3. Celebrate any time you reach a goal no matter how small and it will

reinforce your positive attitude for future goals.

In the next chapter we will be exploring one way to generate a stream of income.

Chapter Twenty Five – Start a Business

One of the best ways to create a stream of income is by starting a business. There are numerous ways to set up a business including starting from scratch, buying a franchise, buying an existing business or join a network marketing company. Although an existing system is in place, buying a franchise or an existing business will require a significant amount of investment dollars. In these two cases, you will need to research the company and financial statements extensively to make an intelligent decision. Starting from scratch can work, but you need a great idea, the knowledge and the funds to develop the business. In this case, a lot of time will be spent organizing as well as a heavy expenditure on marketing the product, idea or service.

The least expensive alternative and a great place to start, is by getting involved in a network marketing opportunity. Not only will it have a system, products and/or services in place but it will also provide the education and training to make you successful. Most of these type of businesses cost very little to get involved. Just a word of caution though, if you want to be truly successful, you have to be prepared to work hard at it. The rewards are worth the effort. The very nature of network marketing will create multiple streams of both passive and active income.

For the reasons above, network marketing is the fastest growing type of business in the world. It allows anyone, even those with no experience, the opportunity to learn and grow a business without the excessive cost of start ups. There are literally hundreds of different products and services to choose from and you will surely find something that you are interested in. The key is to find a product or service that you believe in and you can be completely committed to. This way your passion for the product or service itself will be passed on to customers and your team.

The company takes care of delivery, accounting and administration and you will still be able to write off certain expenses of doing business against the income generated. When joining the business, you will be the down-line of the individual bringing you in. This up-line will provide you with the necessary guidance to become successful. They are extremely interested in your success. The premise is if you make money, they make money. They provide you with the system plan and when adhered to, it becomes almost fool-proof. The law of numbers is very significant in network marketing and the Pareto principle or the 80/20 rule will become evident. This means for every 10 people you talk to, 8 will say "No" and 2 will say "Yes". Also, the law of numbers works here, the more people you talk to, the more will say "Yes".

In network marketing, there are generally two ways to create income. The first way is to sell the products or services and receive commissions on sales (active and passive income). The second way is to recruit a team, your personal down-line. You will receive commissions on their sales and so on (passive income).

Is it possible to sell products and / or services and receive both active and passive income? Yes, let's use a financial services company for example. Say you sold your client some Segregated Funds. If the sale was paid for with a lump sum, you will receive active income (commission on the one-time payment). Instead we set up, what we discussed earlier, a dollar cost averaging purchase of the Segregated Fund and the client purchases units every month. Now the first month of commissions paid is active income and every subsequent month after becomes passive income. The work was done on the first month and now the income comes in every month without activity on your part.

The passive income from recruiting is a result of the team members making sales and providing their up-line, that's you, with commissions from those sales. Again, income created without you having to labor. You still will have to provide some type of activity such as training of your down-line or client follow ups but these, primarily, will be used to generate more sales.

Chapter Summary

There are several ways to start a business but the least expensive and the best for someone who has limited knowledge, is to join a network marketing company. It is of upmost importance that you find a product or service that you believe in and are committed to. In these types of arrangements, income is obtained in basically two ways either through personal sales or sales generated by your recruited down-line.

Below is your action list for this chapter;
1. Do some research into the various network marketing opportunities and find a product or service that you could be committed to.
2. If you look towards a Financial Services company you will be able to get involved in a business and increase your comprehension of this book.
3. For an opportunity described in 2 above, contact the author using the appendix in the book.

The next two chapters are directly related to network marketing and more importantly, further strategies of the wealthy. The first chapter further reinforces the premise that you cannot do it alone. While the other is the life blood of any business and without it there would be no growth or income.

Chapter Twenty Six – Other Peoples Time

The playing field is level for everyone, as we all only have 24 hours in any given day. Seeing as we are restricted to that, how can we do more during that time? The answer is to use other people's time. Why would other people be willing to assist us? The answer to that is they will be helping themselves as well. This is the basic employee and employer relationship. To achieve your goals sooner, we will need to have other people help us get there. This concept was explained in the chapter on team building. We compensate our professionals with our business and/or money for their services. Our inner circle is compensated by the sharing of mutually beneficial information and service.

In network marketing, our up-line guides us and when we are successful they will be compensated by receiving their share of commissions from our sales. Our down-line does the same for us and we benefit from their sales. The magic occurs when we compound their efforts just like compound interest. Our down-line will then recruit their down-line and we now benefit from both our immediate down-line and their down-line and their down-lines down-line and so on.

There are two ways to magnify this income potential, by building wide and/or deep. Building wide means to try and develop as many legs as possible or direct down-lines. Building deep means to take the direct down-line or leg and have them develop down lines and so on (see the diagram below). The combination of these two magnifiers will expand your business and therefore your income. An important item to note here is that although there is the potential to make a great deal of money through recruiting, everyone will have to sell the products or services in order for compensation to be paid.

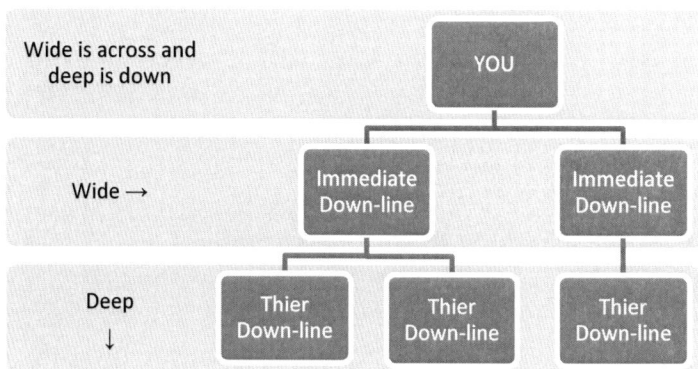

Wide is across and deep is down		YOU	
Wide →	Immediate Down-line		Immediate Down-line
Deep ↓	Thier Down-line	Thier Down-line	Thier Down-line

The potential for making income is only restricted by the lack of development of your down-line. By you assisting your recruits in developing their recruits and so on, affects what you will receive. If you want to grow your business, you must assist every level of your down-line to develop their own.

Chapter Summary

To reach your goals you will need to make use of other people's efforts and time. In network marketing, you will learn to compound other people's effort in order to increase your own income. This compounding of peoples time can be used in any business and is not restricted to network marketing. Building teams wide as well as deep is the key to exponential growth.

Below is your action list for this chapter;
1. You should now be involved in a network marketing organization. Make sure you first become a product expert.
2. Now start building a team by developing an immediate down-line.
3. Once you have three immediate recruits, start helping them go deep.

We have explored compounding other people's time and efforts, but as mentioned above, we need to sell the product or services. The next chapter will deal with that word that sends shivers down most people's spines, "Sales".

Chapter Twenty Seven – Sales

Sales are the lifeblood of any business, without it there would be no growth and there would be no business. Even though you are not cognizant of the fact, you conduct the act of selling every day, everybody does. Every time we scold a child, we are selling them on the idea of proper behavior. When we go to the gym to work out, we have been sold on the idea that exercise will make us fit, feel better and improve our bodies. So it makes sense that if you want to do well in any business venture that you need to develop your selling skills. The best way to do this is practice.

Network marketing will require that you practice selling not only the products and/or services but also recruiting team members. So it is important that you become very familiar with the product / service and commit to it through personal use. It's much easier to make presentations when you yourself are a customer. If you can provide your own personal testimony, in addition to other customer testimonies or referrals, this will go a long way to persuading a new customer to take part. So, get to know the product intimately, invest the time to learn all the answers.

As you may recall, the two ways that money is made in network marketing is through personal sales or down-line team members (recruiting) making sales (trails). Trails are the commissions owing to you from the sales of your down-line. You can make good money from personal sales (finite because of your time) but you can make a fortune from the sales of your team members (infinite). Again, your personal sales are active income and passive income and your team sales are strictly passive income.

Selling is a numbers game, the more people you speak to, the more clients you will get. Get used to hearing no, don't let it discourage you. As a matter fact, get excited, as the more no's you get, the closer you are to a yes. Previously, we said that out of 10 you will get approximately 8 that say "no" and 2 that say "yes", even these numbers are aggressive. As you become more experienced, polishing your presentation through practice and knowledge, you will get more saying "yes".

The days of pushing a product onto someone, whether they want it or not, are gone. Customers are much more educated than before and tend to resist being pushed into something they were not looking for in the first place. If they need or want the product and all other things being equal, if they like and trust you then they will get it from you. You should be looked at as a resource person with information on the product or service and have the ability to deliver the same.

When closing the sale, always ask for referrals. It can be worded this way, "Do you know anyone that could benefit from getting the products (service) you received that I could contact to determine their interest?" Ask for at least three names and phone numbers. Help them think about it by discussing groups they belong to such as sports clubs, workmates, personal friends etc.

Once you have customers, it is very important to maintain a relationship with them. The reason for this is that, you will be able to generate more sales from existing customers than you can from new customers. Regular follow-ups should be scheduled discussing questions, product satisfaction and further business.

Chapter Summary

Every day, without realizing, you make a series of pitches or presentations which is in fact selling. Network marketing allows you to practice your presentation skills with the products, services and recruiting. The more that say "No" the closer you are to "Yes". The key is to become trustworthy and likeable. Remember, follow up with your existing customers and always ask for referrals.

Below is your action list for this chapter;
1. Every day, when you wake recite this additional tidbit from Tom Hopkins (Author and Sales Great), "Today, I will meet the right people, at the right

place, at the right time, for the betterment of all!"

2. Learn everything there is to learn about your company's product and/or services.

3. Practice your sales presentation in the mirror and see if you would buy from that person or become a member of their team.

The next three chapters deal with Real Estate investing, the different types, rental income in particular and different ways of financing your purchases.

Chapter Twenty Eight – Real Estate

Real estate is one of those investments that are tangible assets. You can see it, feel it and make improvements to it. If you bought stocks from a publicly traded company and didn't like the way it was run, you couldn't change it. Whereas, if you bought a house to rent out and you wanted to increase the value of it, you could do any number of things to accomplish that, such as paint it, add an addition, do renovations etc.

Some authors differentiate between your personal home and properties that earn income. They maintain that because your home does not earn an income it is not an asset, yet in the eyes of the bank they are an asset. Some types of real estate cost you money each month, like your home or a speculative property (not earning income) whereas some put money in your pocket each month as positive cash flow.

There are many different types of investments in real estate and below we describe a few. We will be focusing on one in particular, in a later chapter. Investments in real estate can include vacant land, developing property, flips, residential property rentals, commercial property rentals and personal living space.

Personal living space can be broken down further to trailers, houses, apartments or condominiums. Basically, any place you are living in. A person does have a choice to rent or buy their living space. Generally, it is better to buy and apply monthly payments to ownership. You will have an asset after paying the mortgage down. The equity you have in the place is considered an asset by the bank. This equity can be used to secure further loans. Equity is the difference between the market value of the property and what the remaining amount owing is. Does this mean if you are renting should you rush out and buy a place to live? Not necessarily, perhaps you are renting at such a low rate and investing the difference that it would not be feasible to buy your own place. Each person has to analyze their own situation.

Investment in vacant land involves buying a piece of land with no buildings or development on it, usually with a speculative intention. You would be hoping that eventually the value will increase, at which time you would sell it for a handsome profit. Although this sounds good, unless you can derive income from the property to pay for monthly expenses, this will create a negative cash flow. In other words, every month that you hold onto this property you will be paying money out of your pocket to maintain it. Examples of expenses can include property taxes, mortgages and maintenance.

Developing property and flips fall into the same category. Developing property involves putting up a structure on vacant land or replacing an existing structure. The resulting property is then either leased out or sold. Flips involve buying an existing structure, renovating and selling it as quickly as possible. Both of these investments will take a significant amount of investment and technical knowledge to be successful. These are best left until you have some experience and gathered sufficient resources.

Rentals, both commercial and residential are covered in the next chapter. Investors first starting out are typically attracted to this form of real estate investing. Regardless of where you start, know that almost all millionaires have invested in real estate in one form or another. The old adage, "they aren't making any more of that stuff" is true. This displays the basics of supply and demand. As population increases, the demand for property increases, because the supply of land does not increase, the price will. There will always be fluctuations in price but the trend is upwards.

Chapter Summary

As a tangible asset, real estate's value can be increased by making improvements on it. Real estate can generate a negative or a positive cash flow. You should focus on property that provides positive cash flow. Real estate profits can be generated through speculation, developing, flipping, and renting.

Although there are ups and downs in the price of real estate, over time it is always on an upward trend. Real estate is almost always a part of a wealthy person's portfolio.

Below is your action list for this chapter;
1. Do you own your personal living space? If yes read 2 and 3, if no go to 4.
2. How can you personally increase the value of the property?
3. Determine what equity you have in the property by calculating the difference between the current market value and the amount owing.
4. Consider buying a place of your own by looking at the prices in your own neighborhood.
5. Calculate the difference in price between renting and buying. Don't forget things like insurance, property taxes and utilities.

The next chapter is on rental properties and the passive income generated by them.

Chapter Twenty Nine – Rental Properties

There are many different forms of rental properties including parking lots, houses, condominiums, apartment blocks, warehouses, retail, industrial etc. Generally, they are classified into two areas, residential and commercial. Rental properties produce passive income. Meaning, once you have tenants, the money comes in regularly without any effort on your part. To be truly passive income, you will require the services of a property manager, who normally will charge in the range of 5-10% of gross receipts. This property manager will take care of all the day to day problems associated to rental properties. They will look after finding renters, arranging maintenance and provide you with the monthly income. The key to being a successful rental property investor is to only buy properties that create a positive cash flow.

This chapter introduces only two types of rental properties, single family dwellings and retail commercial space. Single family dwellings include houses, condominiums and anywhere that a single family can reside. You will have to research what the rents are priced at in the neighborhood that you are looking at. There is a lot more to consider, but the main focus is finding a property that will provide a positive cash flow after all expenses are paid. When first buying a rental property, it is

113

important that you feel comfortable with the type of property and it is suggested you start small. If you have experienced the challenge of living in your own place, this will go a long way to provide you with knowledge and comfort. Start looking for properties in your own neighborhood.

If you conventionally purchase a rental property you will require at least 25% as a down payment and should be able to obtain a standard mortgage for 25 years. To calculate whether or not the property you have found is going to produce a positive cash flow or not, you must subtract from the rental rate, the mortgage payment, the property taxes, the insurance, property manager's fee and maintenance costs. If you are left with any money this will be the positive cash flow. Don't forget that the tenant must pay all utilities. To find this type of property, even with 25% down will take a lot of searching. You may have to look at 100 houses to find 5 candidates and then only one that fits your needs.

You may want to first find a good property manager even before you start looking for your first rental property. A good property manager should be able to inform you of the going rents for the neighborhood you are looking in. Once you do find the right property, inform the property manager of your interest in it and ask them to look for a tenant. Tell them that you wish to personally look through the candidate's application, after the property manager has done their checks. Finding the right tenant is especially important in residential properties.

Make sure your property manager knows that you require the first month rent, last month rent and damage deposit. Make the damage deposit a different amount than the rent. Let's say the rent is $1,000 per month, ask for $2000 for first and last and an extra $750 for damage deposit. Depending on market conditions, you may have to eliminate the last month's rent. The property manager will guide you as to what the market will bear.

There are pros and cons involved in buying retail commercial space in comparison to residential. In retail space, the renter wishes to attract customers to the premise and will usually spend money on leasehold improvements. These leasehold improvements will enhance the value of the building. As opposed to residential tenants, who generally will not do any improvements and sometimes reduce the value by damaging property. The purchase of retail space is more expensive, as special reports will be required for lenders. These can include commercial appraisal, various inspection and environmental reports. Plus lenders may require more money down and higher interest rates. On the plus side, because commercial properties are more business related sellers will be more conducive to creative financing (more on that later). Commercial property is harder to acquire and is normally harder to sell, but the underlying principle with rental properties is that we invest in them to provide passive income and intend to hold on to them indefinitely.

Any incidental growth from appreciation is a perk of dealing with rental properties. A combination of getting a good price on purchase, mortgage paid by tenants and appreciation presents an opportunity down the road to refinance and take cash out for other investments. We will look at this in more detail in the next chapter.

Chapter Summary

Regardless of which type of rental property you decide to invest in, find a property manager first. A good property manger will provide you with valuable information and peace of mind. There are advantages and disadvantages to single family residential properties and retail commercial properties. Start small and within your comfort zone. Conventional ways of purchasing include funding a down payment and securing financing through a bank or other lender. Positive cash flow is what we are searching for and appreciation is a perk. You make money at the time of purchase, as the strategy is to buy and hold.

Below is your action list for this chapter;

1. Go back to the chapter on building a team and find a good property manager that will work with you.
2. Decide what type of property you wish to invest in and begin researching what the rental rates are.
3. Start looking in the newspapers, contact real estate brokers, talk to your property manager and find properties that fit your needs.
4. When you find something that seems feasible, work out whether or not you will receive a positive cash flow.

Remember that research is of key importance. You will require a lot more information and must feel comfortable before taking the plunge and making an offer. There are other ways of purchasing a property and we will talk about them in the next chapter.

Chapter Thirty – Creative Financing

In the previous chapter, we touched on conventional financing, which is described as placing a standard down payment on property and then financing the remainder through a mortgage with a lending institution such as a bank or trust company. Then creative financing, is really, any deviation from this norm. It can include seller financing, reduced to no down payment, financing from other sources and other combinations. No matter which financing method is chosen, we must produce a positive cash flow after all expenses are accounted for.

Seller financing is often a more economical route, as normally the requirements are much less rigid than financial institutions. There will be no need for inspections and appraisals with residential properties, although they are still recommended. With commercial properties, environmental reports are very expensive as well as appraisals and both are not required when a seller is financing. Appraisals, if not needed for financing, may still provide peace of mind that money offered is relatively close to current market value and inspections will point out any deficiencies. This type of financing allows the amount of down payment to also be adjusted as well as the interest rate and terms of the mortgage. Sometimes it is easier to obtain financing through sellers of commercial property as they may be used to receiving periodic payments from business operations. Whereas, sellers of residential, especially where the seller is living on the premise, need cash to purchase another home in which to live and are less receptive to seller financing. In all cases, it is strategically sound to investigate what the seller is going to do with proceeds.

When buying any investment property, try to reduce the amount of personal cash invested to as close to zero as possible and still maintain a positive cash flow. Using personal cash to fund the down payment will increase the equity and also may increase cash flow but almost always will reduce the R.O.I. (return on investment). On the other hand, any reduction in the amount of financing, whether it is for the mortgage or the down payment will result in an increase in positive cash flow.

Another way to reduce the amount of personal cash used in a purchase is to take on partners. By doing this, you will be able to maintain the positive cash flow but of course will have to split it with your partners. Another way to reduce your input of personal cash is to borrow the down payment and pay it back with the positive cash flow. Alternatively, you could ask the seller to finance a portion of the down payment, making payments with the positive cash flow.

Banks and trust companies are not the only way to finance your purchase. We previously mentioned that you could take on a partner and that they could finance the purchase. Another alternative is to make contact with a mortgage broker. They have access to numerous lenders willing to finance and no allegiance to any particular one. A lot of these lenders can be private individuals looking to invest their money in mortgages secured by properties. Yet another alternative is find those willing to finance by enquiring with friends, family or even advertise the amount you require and what you are willing to offer. Finally, you can combine any of the ideas above as you are only restricted by your own creativity.

Chapter Summary

There are many different ways to finance the purchase of property and you are only restricted by your personal creativity. You must make sure after all expenses, including financing, that you are creating a positive cash flow. Using the least amount of personal cash and the most of other people's money (OPM), will put money in your pocket. Search for a means of creative financing even before you select a property and this will be like prequalifying at a bank.

Below is your action list for this chapter;

1. Go to the bank you are dealing with, tell them what you are doing and ask to get prequalified for loan amounts, terms and rates.
2. Do the same with a mortgage broker as you did with your bank.
3. Search other creative financing methods at your disposal and figure out where and how much you can get together.

Real estate deals with tangible assets, whereas there are other areas where money can be made with intangible assets such as the stock market. This is the focus of the next chapter.

Chapter Thirty One – Stock Investing

The purpose of this chapter is to introduce you to the stock market and to make you aware of the possibility of making money by buying and selling stocks. The basic underlying premise is that in order to make money, you must buy low and sell high, but rarely does this happen to the majority of stock market investors. Why? People tend to buy in when they see a stock rising in price. The fact is, when the price is rising and a buying frenzy has started this is usually the wrong time to buy. This is the greed stage, you see the price going up and you do not want to miss the boat. So instead of making a small profit you hold on for the big money. All of a sudden, the stock starts plummeting and now you hold on because you believe it will go back up. You continue to hold on to it as the price dives past what you paid for it, the beginning of the fear stage. Now you think that the stock price will now go down even further and you sell your position creating a loss. What just happened? You did the opposite, you bought high and sold low.

Short term fluctuations in the stock market are based on fear and greed. Short term prices are largely determined by the actions of the majority of investors. Some stock investment theories dictate that you buy and sell, opposite to what the majority are doing. In other words, when everyone is selling, you buy and when everyone is buying, you sell. This investment strategy, without further research, can have dire consequences, as there may be a reason for the stock movement that is not based on fear and greed. So how can we combat the urge to follow the crowd or to do the opposite? In order to have an edge, when investing in the stocks, you will require due diligence. You will need to invest time into education, research and planning. Professional fund managers spend most of their working careers doing these things. So don't assume that reading this one chapter will be enough for you to go out and make money in the stock market. You will have to invest a great deal of time to become good at it.

Education will include learning from courses and books on the stock market. Most of us will not have the time required to become good at investing and so it is advisable to use the professional fund managers mentioned in the previous paragraph. Most wealthy people use these fund managers in one form or another. We will look at their use in the next chapter.

In order to make intelligent choices of what stocks to purchase, research is required. Research investigates the past, present and future to determine appropriate stock choices. We will just touch on two of the many methods, fundamentals and technical analysis. Fundamental analysis looks at company specific details from the past and present to provide insight on future growth and stability. Details include determining past financial performance by perusing financial statements, management track record, company plans and goals, etc. Technical analysis generally involves studying charts that depict past stock prices to determine past and future trends. These trends will tell us an appropriate time to buy in or sell. Again, these chart patterns are influenced by the short term prices. So you should be looking beyond the short term and focus on long term prices. Some invest using one of these specific methods, but it would prudent to use a combination of both.

A wise plan, for someone who is new to investing in the stock market, is to use the buy and hold philosophy. Looking at the stock market over time, we see that prices always increase. There are always fluctuations up and down, but the trend is always up. When using the buy and hold philosophy, you buy stocks that are fundamentally established (mostly blue chip) and hold them for the long term. You use technical analysis to determine when to buy in and try to ignore sort term fluctuations. For long term investors, you merely hold on to the stock until the desired price is reached. For short term investors, you make use of stop losses to lock in a stated return.

For example, you buy XYZ stock at $20 a share and decide that you want at least 10% of a return which is $2. This calculation ignores brokerage fees which will have to be factored in. As soon as the stock passes $22, you set a stop loss of $22 to sell out the stock, when it comes back down to that price. If the stock comes down to that price, you make 10% on your money. If it carries on upward, you can chase higher profits by moving the stop loss higher.

The use of stop losses can also be used to limit your loss, by predetermining what you are willing to lose and setting the stop loss at that price. In our example above, if you decide you can afford a 20% loss, you would set your stop loss at $16, this is to protect you on a downslide. With proper research and purchasing at the right time, you should be able to restrict your losses and maximize your gains.

As we mentioned in previous chapters, a way of creating cash flow with stocks is to locate ones that pay dividends. In an ideal scenario, you would like to find a stock that pays dividends, is blue chip and has potential for capital gains. A lot of stocks will fill this bill and with proper research you will find the gems that are best for you. If growth is more important to you than dividends and you can handle more risk, then you may have to select stocks that are not blue chip and don't pay dividends. It all depends on your particular game plan or goals.

Another way of generating cash flow is through the selling of options. Basically you offer the right to buy or sell your stock at a certain price, by a certain date. Options are way beyond the scope of this work and even experienced investors tend to shy away from these types of investments.

In order to begin investing, you will require setting up a brokerage account. There are discount brokers and full service brokers. Discount brokers charge very little money for commissions but almost never provide any advice. Full service brokers charge more money for commissions but will provide advice. A word of caution, full service brokers make money on commissions and the more business they do the more money they make, whereas use of discount brokers relies on you to do all the research.

You have often heard of someone providing you with a stock tip. When this happens, realize that most likely the stock is already in the moving up stage (buying high). If you do contemplate buying in, do the research first. In most cases these stock tips end up counterproductive and without research you will rely on emotions. **Never make business decisions based on emotions!** This applies to stocks, real estate and any other type of investment.

Chapter Summary

Buy low and sell high! Short term market fluctuations are largely determined by fear and greed. You can increase your chances of making money in the stock market through education, research and planning. It is a good idea to use professional fund managers while you are learning to invest on your own. Making good stocks picks requires doing a fundamental and technical analysis on the company. The use of stop losses can limit your losses as well as lock in your gains. Never invest because of a stock tip. In your search for the ideal stocks, look also for cash flow through dividends.

Below is your action list for this chapter;
1. Set up a discount brokerage account.
2. Don't buy any stock until you have read a couple of books and/or taken some courses.
3. Start looking around at some companies you believe would make good investments and when you find one, do the research.

The next chapter will describe investments that you can make now by using professional fund managers.

Chapter Thirty Two - Mutual Funds, Segregated Funds and ETFs

When first becoming involved as an investor in the stock market, mutual funds, segregated funds and exchange traded funds (ETFs) are a great place to start. Essentially, investors pool their money and a professional manages the fund. This fund manager does the research and invests in companies that fit the investment focus of the fund. This means that individual investors have no input as to how the funds are invested. This does not alleviate your responsibility of research before you invest, as there are thousands of funds to choose from.

This definition of a mutual fund is taken from Investopedia, "An investment vehicle that is made up of a pool of funds collected from many investors for the purpose of investing in securities such as stocks, bonds, money market instruments and similar assets. Mutual funds are operated by money managers, who invest the fund's capital and attempt to produce capital gains and income for the funds investors. A mutual fund's portfolio is structured and maintained to match the investment objectives stated in its prospectus." This definition of a mutual fund can also be used for segregated and exchange traded funds.

There are a few key areas within the definition that are worth going over. The idea of pooling funds allows smaller investors to share in the advantages of being a major investor. These money managers or professional fund managers have years of education and experience behind them. Investigating the fund manager's track record is one of the most important indicators of how a fund will perform. Other research, concerns the fund itself, such as comparing historical performance and perusing the prospectus (details of the fund). Newspapers frequently list all the mutual funds available and this is a good place to start your research.

Generally, segregated funds are the same as mutual funds, but with some important differences. Segregated funds, also called Individual Variable Insurance Contracts (IVICs), are products sold through insurance companies. As a result, you can name a designated beneficiary which bypasses probate and estate taxes. Investment in segregated funds also provides a guarantee of 75 to 100 % of your initial investment if held for a stated period of time, usually 10 years. So let's say you invest $1000 in 2013 and in 2023 the market value of your investment is $695, if you were to sell and had the 100% guarantee you would receive $1000 (your initial investment). You can reset your investment amount at any time but will start the vesting period over again. So in our example above, let's say in 2015 the market value had risen to $1400 and you reset the investment then. As a result, in 2025 the guarantee will provide you $1400 if you sell and the market value is lower. Segregated funds otherwise provide the same benefits as mutual funds. Both mutual and segregated funds have MERs, Management Expense Ratios, and they tend to be slightly higher with segregated funds. These are fees charged by the fund manager for management of the fund and are deducted from the price of the fund and lower the return or growth.

There are sales charges that are normally charged when buying mutual or segregated funds. No load funds do not charge a sales charge but generally have higher MERs. Front load funds charge a sales charge when you buy the fund and back load funds charge a sales charge when you sell your shares. Although a lot of back load funds are set up with a declining sales charge. A declining sales charge reduces for each year you hold the fund shares and will eventually be eliminated. Declining sales charges, reinforces the buy and hold philosophy and motivates investors to hold the investment at least until the sales charge dissipates. You can purchase mutual funds from anyone that holds a mutual fund license. Segregated funds are purchased from separate insurance companies or agents.

ETFs are very similar to the funds discussed above and can be bought and sold through the stock exchange through a broker. This attractive feature makes this investment very liquid. Meaning, sales charges are replaced by a broker's commission when either buying or selling. The MERs are quite small, in comparison to mutual or segregated funds. ETFs can provide both income in the way of distributions and the opportunity for capital gains. Normally, the fund invests in companies to mimic commodity, index or bond prices. Exchange traded funds will fluctuate in price like the rest of the stock market. Segregated and mutual funds prices are calculated at the end of every day, this is called the NAV or Net Asset Value.

The couch potato strategy is an excellent technique for building a growth oriented portfolio. It involves purchasing ETFs that mimic the market indexes. This will reinforce the buy and hold strategy as well as the thought that in the long run, the stock continues an upward trend. Not only will this strategy reduce costs mentioned above but also provide better growth than most of the other funds.

All the investments, mentioned above, can be used for your emergency funds, RRSP, TFSA and extra investments. The fact that they are already managed by professionals will dramatically reduce the time you need to qualify individual investments. When researching ETFs look at past financial performance, when looking at the other funds focus on management.

Chapter Summary

Small investors pool their money, to take advantage of benefits afforded to large institutional investors. The biggest advantage is the use of professional money managers and is a common trait of mutual funds, segregated funds and exchange traded funds. Mutual funds can be purchased through anyone holding a mutual fund license, segregated funds must be purchased from insurance companies and ETFs are purchased on the stock exchanges through brokers. Segregated funds allow for the designation of beneficiaries and provide a guarantee on your investment. ETFs have lower costs to acquire and manage than the other funds. All the funds are very liquid and can be cashed out relatively quickly. These would be great investments for your RRSPs and TFSAs.

Below is your action list for this chapter;
1. Try to locate a newspaper listing of mutual funds so that you may review and compare their performance.
2. Contact an insurance agent to discover what segregated funds they have available and/or contact the author through the appendix.
3. Do some internet research on ETFs, start by looking at the Toronto Stock Exchange and look at the ETFs listed on it.

4. All these different funds can be purchased using dollar cost averaging. Do your research, select an appropriate investment and start contributing.

The next chapter focuses on what bonds are and the benefits of investing in them.

Chapter Thirty Three – Bonds

Again, we use Investopedia, to provide you with the definition of a bond, "A debt investment in which an investor loans money to an entity (corporate or governmental) that borrows the funds for a defined period of time at a fixed interest rate. Bonds are used by companies, municipalities, states and U.S. and foreign governments to finance a variety of projects and activities." In Canada, when mentioning bonds, we immediately think of "Canada Savings Bonds". These are extremely safe, low risk investments, but also provide a very low growth or interest rate.

Bonds should be incorporated into your portfolio as they can be extremely safe and liquid. They provide interest income as well as capital gains. On an initial offering, bonds are sold at face value with stated rate of interest. This interest can be paid out regularly or it can be compounded. The interest is taxed at your top marginal rate. Bonds can also be traded on a secondary market. Depending on the bond rating and interest rate, it will sell for a premium or a discount on the face value. That is they will sell for more or less than the original face value. If a bond is held to maturity or resold prior to maturity, any difference between purchase price and selling price will be a capital gain or loss.

Some mutual funds and segregated funds will already have a mix of bonds integrated into their asset mix to provide growth and safety. Some ETFs invest exclusively in bonds and provide investors with income. Not all bonds are safe and not all bonds provide low growth. Bonds are rated based on risk and it stands to reason that the more risk involved with a bond the more it should pay for growth. When bonds become very risky they are usually dubbed as "junk bonds". Unless you have vast experience with bonds, we suggest that you stay away from junk bonds.

Just like stocks it is important that you research who is offering the bonds. Generally, safer bonds are offered by governments including federal (Canada Bonds), municipals, etc. Utility companies and corporate bonds offer higher rates, but require that you research the companies to look for stability, growth and a track record. Until you gain sufficient experience and knowledge, stick to mixes included in mutual, segregated funds or ETFs.

This may be a good time to introduce Promissory Notes, which are very similar to bonds. Promissory notes are also debt instruments that are issued by individuals, companies or any type of entity. They allow the issuer to secure funds through mutually agreed terms which include interest rate, schedule of payments and consequences of default of payment. Investing in these can be very risky, make sure you do your homework.

These are a great way to use OPM, (other people's money), for your own investment purposes. You can even secure these with the investment you are using the funds for. An example would be to issue a promissory note to obtain funds for the purchase of property and using that property as collateral to secure the loan.

Chapter Summary

Both bonds and promissory notes are debt instruments that provide investors with interest income. Bonds also provide the opportunity for capital gains when traded on a secondary market. Regardless of how safe these investments appear, you must do your homework and investigate the entity providing these instruments. Promissory notes are an excellent way for you to use OPM and secure funds for investing.

Below is your action list for this chapter;
1. Review your investments and determine whether or not you are already involved in bonds. Look in particular, at mutual and segregated funds to see whether your mix of assets includes bonds.
2. When shopping for funds, determine whether they contain a bond component.

3. Locate suitable bond ETFs and research their track record and consider investing in them.
4. Look further into using Promissory Notes as a means of using OPM. Search the internet or other sources to locate a template for a promissory note and edit it to suit your purposes.

Not all that glitters is gold. The next chapter will introduce commodity investing and when done properly can provide moderate safety and high growth.

Chapter Thirty Four – Commodities

Once again, we start with a definition, a commodity, as described by Dictionary.com is, "1. An article of trade or commerce, especially a product as distinguished from a service. 2. Something of use, advantage, or value. 3. Stock Exchange. Any unprocessed or partially processed good, as grain, fruits, and vegetables, or precious metals." There several ways of investing in commodities including trading on a commodity exchange, purchasing actual product or investing in a commodity ETF.

Trading on a commodity exchange is not only risky but requires quite a bit of extra knowledge on how the exchange works and the commodity you will be trading. In order to set up a commodity trading account, an investor requires a certain amount of net worth and a good credit rating. Unlike the stock market, where you can only lose the amount of money you have invested, a loss in the commodity market requires repayment up to the value of the contract. This loss can be controlled by the effective use of stops, but sometimes gaps in prices, can defeat these stop losses. The upside of commodity exchange is that you are only required to put down 5-10% of the entire contract. This allows the use of OPM to significantly magnify your return on investment. This type of investing is not recommended for novice investors and even seasoned investors tend to shy away because of the risk.

Investing, by actually buying the product, allows the physical holding of commodities. A good example for this is buying coins or bullion, the most common being gold and silver. There are two problems with investing this way. Gold, for example, may be priced at $2000 an ounce but if you buy bullion (bars and wafers) you will pay a sales charge. If you buy coins, the price will be higher because of processing. Secondly, you will have storage costs to contend with, like buying a safe and having it installed or renting a safety deposit box at a bank. Still, it does provide security in that the coins or bullion are accepted worldwide regardless of the economy or state of affairs at home. For this reason, you might consider holding a very small portion, 1 - 5% of your portfolio, in coins or bars of Gold or Silver.

Commodity ETFs provide a great way to invest in commodities and have one of those professional money managers look after it for you. The value of the ETFs, mimic the price of the commodity. For example, when the price of gold is up, then a <u>Bull</u> ETF for gold will also be up whereas a <u>Bear</u> ETF will be down. Let's clarify a few points from this last sentence such as what a "Bull" is and what a "Bear" is. First of all, "bull" means that prices are going up or we are in a growth period whereas "bear" means that prices are going down or we are having a recession in prices. The second thing you should have noticed is that ETFs can have two faces one ETF mimics prices going up and the other mimics prices going down. So, before investing do some research and determine whether prices are going to increase or decrease. Then make a choice accordingly. Keep in mind, if prices continually rise over the long run, a long term strategy is to hold bull ETFs whereas, if prices are projected to go down, gains may be obtained by holding bear ETFs for the short term.

Chapter Summary

Commodity or futures trading on commodity exchanges can be very risky. Novice investors should stick to buying tangible commodities such as gold and silver and investing in ETFs. ETFs mimic prices going up and down. Generally, if you are using the buy and hold concept you should invest in bull ETFs. If buying gold and silver bullion or coins, restrict your investment to 1 - 5% of the total value of your portfolio.

Below is your action list for this chapter;
1. Obtain a safety deposit box from your bank. The rent is charged on a yearly basis and if holding financial papers in this box, you can deduct

the cost as a carrying charge on your tax return.

2. Until you obtain more knowledge and experience stay away from trading on a commodity exchange.
3. Determine the value of your portfolio and calculate what 5% of it equals to and consider buying some gold or silver coins to place in the safety deposit box.
4. Investigate the different commodity ETFs available and consider becoming involved in one.

We are going back now to developing you and your character. A wise woman once said, "You can have all the money in the world, but what good is it if you don't live long enough to enjoy it?" **Anny Lautischer**.

Chapter Thirty Five – Health, Fitness and Nutrition

You must try to seek a balance in your life. Your time should be split between looking after yourself, spending time with family and becoming financially independent. Someone once said, "Wherever you are, be there!" Meaning when you are with family concentrate on them and when you are at work concentrate on work etc.

It is of upmost importance that you look after yourself first, this enables you to look after and help others. When flying, the preflight instructions given by the flight attendant, details that when the oxygen masks are released out of the overhead compartment, first put on yours and then put on your children's. Why, because without you being ok first, you will be of no use to them.

Health can be broken down several ways including physical, mental and emotional. In this chapter, we will be dealing with the physical portion. The whole purpose of physical health is to increase your longevity and enhance your quality of life. Unfortunately, too many people go to see doctors in the reactive stage. That is, when something is wrong, we go to the doctor to cure or help us. We spend far less time going to them for proactive help, such as routine checkups to try and locate problems that have not yet surfaced.

Many illnesses, if diagnosed before symptoms become apparent, are manageable and even curable. Examples include prostate problems or breast cancer, which detected early enough, can be dealt with and not affect overall quality of life and longevity. At the very least, a person should attend the doctor's office once a year to have a full physical and while there enquire as to what other type of checkups are a good idea. The older you become the more checks are needed but an ounce of prevention is worth a pound of cure. To enhance our lives and our health, in addition to regular checkups, we should focus on fitness and nutrition.

There are varying degrees of fitness that a person can achieve, depending on the time and energy expended. It is extremely important for your safety that you consult with a doctor before starting any exercise program. There are many different forms of exercise. Benefits from exercise include a more efficient cardiovascular system, increase strength, body tone, and flexibility. Specific exercise methods will focus more on these areas, such as jogging for cardiovascular improvement, weightlifting for strength, and stretching for flexibility. Almost all types of exercise will assist in body toning and esthetics.

The key to starting an exercise program is not to overdo your initial workouts or burnout mentally by doing too much. An exercise program should be designed around you, taking into account your goals and your present fitness levels. Just like business, you should seek out a professional fitness consultant to prepare a program for you. A good start is to do 30 minutes a day at least three times a week, with a combination of stretching, running or walking and light exercises such as push-ups and sit-ups. As your fitness level increases so should your level of commitment. This should be achieved by a steady gradient with the goal of conducting workouts 60 minutes a day, six days a week.

A sample program could consist of one day of cardiovascular training, the next day of weight training and stretching both days. When looking for improvement, don't look for it from the scale. Your fitness consultant should be able to test you upon initial contact and then periodically, every three months, to measure your improvement.

An important part of your exercise regime is going to include watching what you eat. A major portion of your fitness goals will be affected by your eating habits. There is a plethora of fad diets out there that a person could try. The problem with most diets is that people reach a desired goal and then stop the diet. They then revert back to their previous diet, ending up where they started or worse. A good way to start paying attention to your eating habits is by reading labels, try to stay away from fat rich foods and definitely stay away from junk foods. Avoid saturated fats. Eating smaller portions and more meals will go a long way to keeping hunger pains away and the consumption of fewer calories. Drink plenty of water, at least 1 to 2 liters a day. Do not eat anything within 2-3 hours before bed.

Someone who exercises quite vigorously will require a lot of protein rich food, but be careful as most protein rich food, meat in particular, carries a lot of bad cholesterol as well. Foods that help lower cholesterol are mostly obtained from non-meat sources, such a fish oils, fiber, specific grains and vegetables. Once again, your fitness consultant should have knowledge on nutrition or should be able to refer you to a sports nutritionist to help you plan your dietary needs.

Chapter Summary

A combination of regular doctor check-ups, exercise and diet will enhance your life and promote your overall health. Consult a doctor before starting any exercise program. Do not overdo your initial workouts to prevent burn out. Consult a fitness professional to set up an exercise plan specifically designed for you. Stay away from fatty foods and drink plenty of water.

Below is your action list for this chapter;
1. Make an appointment with your doctor for a full physical and at the

same time advise them that you are going to begin an exercise program.

2. Seek out a fitness consultant that can test you and develop a program specifically designed for you.
3. Start reading food labels and reduce your intake of fatty foods. Stop eating junk food and don't eat within 3 hours of going to bed.
4. Add another two chants to recite every day, when you wake: from Tom Hopkins (Author and Sales Great), "I'm alive! I'm awake! And I feel great!" and "I feel good. I feel fine. I feel this way all the time!
5. Set some fitness goals for yourself.

When you achieve your fitness goals, reward yourself, one way is by showing off your new body on a holiday to a warm spot. In the next chapter, we will discuss those things that you should avoid showing off.

Chapter Thirty Six – Status Symbols

It is never wise to flaunt your success when you have made it to your goals. If one of your goals was to get that special car or the big house on the hill then that is reasonable. You know you have reached your goals, it is not necessary to publicly display your wealth. Yes you will see those who come into money displaying their good fortune but most millionaires, who worked to get there, keep a very low profile. The ones that normally display their wealth for all to see have won the money, inherited it or have borrowed it.

Yes most of those that drive the fancy cars, live in the big houses and have all the toys are living way beyond their means. They have borrowed the money to pay for the stuff and/or have high paying jobs and low net worth. They have a lot in common with those that win the money, in that they both are buying those things that they believe will identify them as being wealthy. Eventually either the money runs out or the debt becomes unmanageable. These people that are living beyond their means are really trying to fool everyone and themselves into believing they have made it. This does not happen all the time but in most cases.

Those that win the money or that inherit it, normally just magnify what they were before. For example, if you were bad with money before, you will be terrible with more money.

Most people that win or inherit money will spend it all and have nothing again after a period of time. The only exceptions are those that have common sense before getting the new funds and actually plan how to keep it or make more. Those that have to make their own way tend to manage their money much better when they start getting a surplus of it.

Here is the difference between the two types of people. Those that win it or inherit it and lose it don't normally know how to get it back. Those that make their own way can lose it all and get it back again. They will probably get even more as they have experienced learning opportunities and discovered the path to wealth.

Most millionaires live in average neighborhoods, drive average cars and wear mediocre clothing. From the outside their lives look very boring and exactly the opposite of what the media depicts as rich. You may find out that these people are rich because of word of mouth or perhaps by a generous gift made to a charity, but for the most part you will have a hard time picking them out of the crowd.

If the media would report on most of the millionaires that lead these discreet lives, everyone else would be shocked to discover that perhaps the neighbor down the street is a millionaire. The media is in the business of selling newspapers or promoting their individual type of media and as a result will focus on super rich and those that flaunt it.

Those who are lime lighted in the media lose all their privacy and are inundated with people looking for hand outs.

By being discreet with your success, you avoid a lot of extra problems plaguing those mentioned above. You will be able to maintain privacy and security in knowing you are not a target for criminals and those who wish to share in your success. When it benefits you to let others know of your success you should consider passing the information along. For instance, let us say that you are a financial planner and your goal is to help other people become financially independent. Letting them know where you came from and what you have achieved, shows them that you can talk the talk and walk the walk. Personally, you want a financial planner, who has made it themselves, to guide you as to how to get there.

Chapter Summary

When you work towards your financial goals and achieve them, you tend to watch the way you spend your money. Those that display their wealth usually have either won the money, inherited it or are in debt and unless they are smart, this display will only be for the short term. Those that have reached financial independence, through their efforts, tend to hold onto it much longer and don't squander it on shiny things. If by chance, they lose their wealth, making it back again is possible.

Below is your action list for this chapter;
1. Never borrow money to purchase displays of wealth (bad credit).
2. If it benefits you to let people know of your success, do it through communication not through status symbols.
3. Do you have any displays of wealth? Consider why you have them.
4. Remember, this does not include any item that may be one of your goals to acquire. These are really rewards for reaching your goals.

Two traits, that are learnable, are the topic of the next chapter and essential for the development of your character and your fortune.

Chapter Thirty Seven – Honesty and Integrity

The Webster's Ninth New Collegiate Dictionary defines "Integrity" as, "an unimpaired condition", "firm adherence to a code of moral values, incorruptibility", "the quality or state of being complete or undivided, completeness". We see that honesty and integrity are intertwined in the description of "honesty" found from the same reference, "HONESTY implies a refusal to lie, steal, or deceive in any way; INTEGRITY implies trustworthiness and incorruptibility to a degree that one is incapable of being false to a trust, responsibility or pledge;" Other words used, include probity and honor.

The development of these characteristics will go a long way to generate trust and motivate people to want to be associated to you. It is easier than you think to be able to develop these qualities. It will require you to be conscious of whatever you say and do and make sure it is the right thing. When you tell someone or indicate that you will do something or make a promise, then do it. You will attract people with the same qualities you project. So if you project honor, honesty and integrity then people with these traits will be attracted to you.

An ideal thought to walk around with, is to leave this world in a better place than the way you found it. Meaning that you try to do more than just what you need to get by. For example, you are walking down a sidewalk, en route to a trash can carrying trash and you spot a candy wrapper on the ground. You swoop down, pick up the wrapper and deposit both in the can. You just made the world a better place than you found it. This is why a lot of people join a service group, to make a difference.

If you strive to do the right thing and work at always being honest, people will gravitate towards you. You will find, especially in business, people will want to deal with you. Your reputation of fair and honest dealing will win you the loyalty of business acquaintances and prospective clients. Anytime you make any kind of decision, take a moment to think whether it is the right thing to do and always go in the right direction.

You are in a checkout line at the grocery store and just realized you are $20 short for the goods you are purchasing. Just at that moment, the person in front of you has pulled money out of their pocket and didn't notice that they dropped $40. They still have enough in their hands to pay for their purchases. You

    a. Pick up the $40 and discreetly put it in your pocket.

    b. You kick it to the side and wait until they are gone and then pick it up.

    c. You ask them to borrow $20 and if they agree, you give them $20 back if they don't agree you keep it all.

d. You pick up the money, pocket $20 and tell them they dropped $20.
e. **The right answer:** You pick up the money give it back to them and then put your items back on the shelf.

By developing your character and furthering your education, you change the world. This domino effect, benefits yourself, serves to enhance the lives of those people that you touch and promotes your credibility. It all starts with the desire to improving yourself and the world around you.

Chapter Summary

To make the world a better place, you must start by improving yourself and developing your character. In developing your character, the traits of upmost importance include honesty and integrity. You generally attract people with the traits you project. Leave the world in a better state than you found it.

Below is your action list for this chapter;
1. Wherever possible make the world a better place than you found it.
2. Any time you make a decision, think and make sure you are doing the right thing.
3. Avoid dishonest and disreputable people.

The next chapter talks about other specific ways in which we can make the world a better place.

Chapter Thirty Eight – Tithing and Charity

Tithing, is much like paying yourself, you provide a percentage of money coming in, for charitable purposes. The percentage amount was traditional set at 10% but it can be any amount. By using a percentage, you can start right now, regardless of whether you are affluent or not. No matter what percentage a person uses to start, you are making the world a better place. If you wait until you are affluent, you will not develop the discipline when the amounts are small, which will make it very difficult to part with the money later.

You are sure to have heard the saying, "What goes around comes around." By providing for the less fortunate, you are in fact ensuring your future, peace of mind and of upmost importance, improving the world. A couple of philanthropists come to mind, one from the late 1800s and one from modern times. Both are considered among the richest men of their times and yet gave a tremendous amount of money to make this a better world.

Andrew Carnegie, born poor in Dunfermline, Scotland in the 1800s, spent half his life making a fortune and then the other half giving it all away. You will see his name everywhere today; Carnegie Hall, Carnegie Libraries, etc. At the beginning of the 1900s he had amassed over 400 million dollars, a sizeable sum even by today's standards and then he gave it all away. Our modern day example is Bill Gates, one of the richest men on the planet. Mr. Gates has already given away hundreds of millions of dollars to charities and he is still in the top ranks of the affluent.

We are only here for a defined period of time and you may not be remembered for being a wealthy person, but you will be remembered for making a difference by giving both of yourself and your money. Andrew Carnegie (Steel Magnate and philanthropist) wrote, "… surplus wealth should be considered as a sacred trust to be administered by those into whose hands it falls, during their lives, for the good of the community."

Once again, do the research before tithing your money to a charitable organization. Even ones that you may be affiliated with, ask what the money is used for, where does it go, how much actually makes it to the end user, etc. There are enough organizations out there, so choose those that provide a tax deduction as they will have more stringent reporting requirements and obviously will provide you with a way to minimize taxes.

We can also benefit our community by not only providing funds but also providing our time. Contributions of one's time, towards bettering the community, is another way of making the world a better place than you found it. There are numerous organizations that are in existence to provide for the communities and are staffed by volunteers that not only provide their time but also their money.

One of these is the Rotary, which has numerous projects benefiting not only the communities in which they are located but also the rest of the world. The Rotary concludes every meeting with "The Four-Way Test" "Of the things we think, say or do
1. Is it the TRUTH?
2. Is it FAIR to all concerned?
3. Will it build GOODWILL and BETTER FRIENDSHIPS?
4. Will it be BENEFICIAL to all concerned?"

When you reach higher levels of financial success, you might consider starting your own charitable organization. This enables you to provide funds and resources where you believe they will do the most good. By doing this, you can also ensure that funds provided make it to the intended targets.

Chapter Summary

Tithing requires that you provide a percentage of money coming in for the donation to charity. Not only can you provide funds but you can also provide your time. Help yourself through Karma, "What goes around comes around". Combined with the previous chapter information, tithing and giving your personal time, your world and everyone else's world will become a better place.

Below is your action list for this chapter;
1. Start tithing today. Begin by allocating 5% of money coming in for charity. (This does not come out of your PYF)
2. Investigate what community service groups are in your area and attend a meeting at each.
3. Research what charities you would be interested in donating to. Follow the money trail and find out where it all goes.
4. Consider what your own charitable organization would be like.
5. Make "giving" another goal of yours.

In the next chapters, we discuss how to catapult your financial goals and achieve exponential growth.

Chapter Thirty Nine – Service of Many

As the title suggests, begin thinking of ways to help lots of people. The more people you help, the more you will benefit. Zig Ziglar (motivational speaker and author) says, "You can have everything in life you want, if you just help other people get what they want." A further quote from the late Jim Rohn (motivational speaker and author) reinforces this sentiment, "Whoever renders service to many puts himself in line for greatness – great wealth, great return, great satisfaction, great reputation, and great joy." We should be cognizant of this thought each time we make plans on achieving our goals. If we focus on servicing the many then the achievement of our goals will require much less effort. Any big successes were the result of service to many.

The place where you can use this philosophy is in the Network Marketing business we mentioned earlier. Make sure your choice of business truly enhances people's lives and then focus to help as many as possible. The more people you contact, the more people you can help, the more you will prosper. This philosophy can also be used in the real estate rental business. By providing housing and / or commercial space for persons or business, you are already providing a valuable service. The next step is to multiply this service through expansion or acquiring more units. By helping others you help yourself. The service of many involves changing your initial focus to the multitude instead of yourself. By doing this you are again making the world a better place than you found it.

Chapter Summary

Although this chapter is brief, the idea is extremely important to our success. We need to change the focus from benefiting ourselves to enhance as many other lives as possible. This change will further your cause to make the world a better place and help achieve your goals quicker.

Below is your action list for this chapter;
1. Determine and commit to paper all the different ways you can serve the multitudes.
2. Add another affirmation to recite every day when you wake, from Tom Hopkins (Author and Sales Great), "Today, I will meet the right people in the right place at the right time for the betterment of all."

The next chapter is also brief, but another way to increase your growth.

Chapter Forty – Think Big

Thinking big is a concept that has the potential to substantially increase your growth but to the inexperienced, it also has the potential to wipe you out in your first investment. Therefore, as suggested previously, start with smaller investments and deals until you gain enough experience before you start going big. There is a difference between thinking big and going big, one is in your thoughts and the other is in your actions.

The underlying thought is that if you are investing or making deals anyway, going big, magnifies the amount of profit. For instance, in buying a piece of real estate, whether you buy a duplex or an apartment block the paperwork or the process is generally the same. Take note of the term, "generally", as there are going to be different items to consider between the two. These items include the amount of startup capital, maintenance costs, what portion of utilities you may be responsible for, eligibility for financing etc. A good thought you should use, when starting out, is taken from the game from Parker Brothers "Monopoly", buy 4 green houses and <u>then</u> 1 red hotel. We should use a gradient system, taking the time to gather experience, knowledge and confidence, before we move on to the big deals.

Any time you use Other People's Money, you are going big. When you invest in stock or other investments and are using leverage, you are going big. You are extending your personal financial resources, to get more and as a result are increasing your risk. You can use the example of buying your own personal living space. In traditional financing, we put money down and obtaining financing in the form of a mortgage. This is a form of thinking big, in that we use OPM to get what we want but in turn we increase our risk. A variation of thinking big, expands on the example above, you buy the biggest place that you are eligible for. Again, you have significantly increased your risk, as you may extend yourself to the limit, but the trade off is that it will also provide you with the biggest place and perhaps the greatest opportunity for appreciation. When investing in stocks and other investments using OPM, you are subjected to the same risk.

You have to examine what is important and what it will take to attain your goals before the concept of thinking and going big is used. Depending on where you have set your goals, you will be using one form or another of thinking big. Donald Trump (real estate magnate and entrepreneur) is quoted, "If you're going to be thinking, you may as well think big."

Chapter Summary

There are different forms or stages of thinking big. To begin with, using OPM is a form of thinking big. After you get the 4 green houses, you get the red hotel is another stage of thinking big. Thinking big and going big are two different actions, always think big. Before going big make sure you have amassed experience, knowledge and confidence. Always evaluate the risk associated with going big.

Below is your action list for this chapter;
1. Go on the internet and locate two properties for sale in your area. This is strictly a fact finding mission. One should be a duplex and one an apartment block. Compare the two and discover what the differences and similarities are.
2. Always think big and do a lot of thinking before going big.

In this chapter, you have been encouraged to think big. In the next chapter we explore using your mind to the fullest.

Chapter Forty One – Mind Power

One of the most important factors that will determine your success in achieving your goals is the proper use of your mind. Proper use includes Mind Set, Positive Mental Attitude and time to think. Your mind is a complex computer that is programmable. Your thoughts can be divided into two sections, conscious and sub-conscious. It is the sub-conscious that you want to program to automate thought and action. You have to program or input good thoughts if you want a good output. You have heard the saying, "garbage in, garbage out". Try to stay away from negative thought processes.

A starting point in the quest for using your mind to the fullest is developing your mind set. If you want to be a millionaire, you have to think and act like a millionaire. First you will have to get rid of preconceived notions on how millionaires act and think. Most Millionaires, as discussed in previous chapters, lead somewhat boring lives as they live well below their means and do not surround themselves with status symbols. They would rather use the money, spent on these trinkets, to invest further. When making decisions, think consciously about how the typical millionaire would handle the situation. You have to believe that you are not only capable of being a millionaire, but that you are already one. By believing in this, your sub-conscious mind will take over and start to provide thoughts automatically. If you are consciously and sub-consciously thinking these thoughts you begin to attract wealth.

You must get rid of negative thoughts and replace them with positive thoughts. This is the basic formula to achieving your goals with a Positive Mental Attitude. Let's clarify, you cannot achieve your goals with just a positive mental attitude, but you cannot achieve your goals without one. A positive mental attitude requires that you remain positive at all times, even during adversity. Find the silver lining in every cloud. When you use a positive mental attitude you will see opportunities not otherwise apparent. By constant use of a positive mental attitude you will attract other positive people and opportunities. This will in turn, program your sub-conscious mind.

Most wealthy people use the next concept and may not even be aware that they are doing it. In order to set your goals and plan your path to achieving them, you need time to think. The following guideline should be used to maximize your potential. First of all, you need to set aside a minimum of 15 minutes every day. Pick a location where you can be alone and get rid of all distractions such as other people, phones, radios, T.V., etc. You will require paper and a pen or pencil. The purpose of these 15 minutes is to make plans, to think about your goals and how you are going to achieve them. Any thoughts that do come up must be committed to paper. Dr. Elmer Gates (teacher, philosopher, inventor), called this "sitting for ideas". He would in fact, sometimes spend hours doing this until he had the answer he was looking for.

Chapter Summary

Mind power involves developing a mind set, incorporating a positive mental attitude and taking the time to think. You must program your sub-conscious mind with the right information to produce a good output. In order to achieve your goals you will require positive thoughts. Sitting for ideas will allow you to develop your action plan.

Below is your action list for this chapter;
1. Following T. Harv Eker's (Author and Motivational speaker) advice will help develop a millionaire mindset. Every time you find money or have received money declare out loud, "I am a money magnet".
2. Add another affirmation to recite every morning from Tom Hopkins (Author and Sales Great), "I see opportunity in every challenge."
3. Schedule at least 15 minutes every day and sit for ideas.

What are you good at? What have you done? How you can use the answers to these questions is the subject of the next chapter.

Chapter Forty Two – Skills and Achievements

Napoleon Hill (Author and motivational Speaker) stated, "Success in its highest and noblest form calls for peace of mind and enjoyment and happiness which come only to the man who has found the work he likes best." To be successful financially as well as mentally, you should discover your talents and perform the ones you enjoy the most. You probably personally know people that make a lot of money and hate what they do. If you really like what you are doing and become an expert at it, the money will follow.

The best way to discover what you truly like is to experience the work first hand. For example before starting your own business in tax preparation, work for a company first to discover if this is something you wish to do. You will gain valuable insight by working for others, without taking a risk. Once you have decided that this is what you want to pursue, focus all your energy towards becoming an expert. This includes study, formal and informal, and gaining experience through working for others and yourself. Let's say you are working at a tax preparers office for eight hours a day, spend an additional hour a day in study on this endeavor. Within a year, you will become an expert and what you lack in natural talent you will make up in acquired skill. If you truly love what you are doing, then spending an extra hour a day in study on the topic will be insignificant.

Let's use one more example, to clarify how to become an expert. This time let's assume you are working a full time job which is not related to the skill you wish to acquire. This method will require a greater sacrifice of your time as you must gain the skills through education and experience outside of your regular hours.

In this example, you wish to own a martial arts school and have no previous experience. The first step is to visit different disciplines, this is a fact finding mission to discover which best fits your needs and wants. Once you have done this, you need to start taking classes in the art selected and spend time outside the class to study. When you reach a certain level, such as your first degree black belt, you can consider yourself good enough to begin teaching. Now in combination with teaching, you must continue study until you become an expert. Now the transition to starting your own school will be easy.

How long would this all take? If you attend classes three times a week and then instruct at least twice a week, it could take as long as five years before starting your own school. So you can see the difference between a full time effort and a part time effort. You may not always get the option to choose which route. If you truly love what you are doing, time is immaterial.

There are times when you must "toot your horn". There is a need to promote your skills and achievements in order to advertise your business. As in the example above, the public needs to know the caliber of the individual instructing. This can be achieved through advertising that you are a black belt, tournaments entered or real life experience. A lot of times, word of mouth is the main means of advertising and as such you must let prospective clients know of your skills and achievements.

To this end, you should begin recording your experience, education and achievements by compiling a "Curriculum Vitae". Why is this done? To influence and persuade the reader, that you are the ideal candidate to suit their needs, whether it is for employment or to convince a prospective client to use your services. When tooting your horn, it should be done in a humble way. You don't want to be considered a braggart, you do want the prospective client to determine that they will benefit by coming to you or your business. The use of status symbols is another example of being a braggart.

Chapter Summary

To become successful, mentally and financially, you must find something you enjoy doing and become an expert at it. Expert status comes from education, experience and focusing your efforts. In order to capture clients and/or customers, they must believe you are the ideal person to provide the product or service to them. All other things being equal, the client must also like and trust you, so don't be a braggart.

Below is your action list for this chapter;
1. Discover what you would like to do.
2. Devote at least one hour every day towards studying on your choice.
3. Try to gain experience in the field of your choice.
4. Focus all your efforts to becoming an expert.
5. Inform prospective clients/customers of your skills and achievements.

Next we will be focusing on the most important people in your life.

Chapter Forty Three – Family First

In an earlier chapter you were told to look after yourself first before you can look after others. To be truly successful in your life, you must strive to achieve a balance between business and family, as the title suggests "family first". When things are good at home, support from your family members will enable you to achieve better results and the path to wealth becomes easier. Without stress and strife in your family life, you can more clearly focus on financial and business goals.

When you are with family, be there and concentrate on family. Adjust your cell phone to take messages and don't give out your home phone number. Aggressively defend your family time and don't let business interfere with it. Most wealthy individuals agree that a balance must be obtained to be able to excel in business and so they place family as their first priority.

If you are married, or have a significant other, it is of upmost importance that you foster and gain the support of that individual in your financial endeavors. They are your first business partner and even though their investment may only be emotional, you'll need their support. This can be accomplished by communicating effectively, efficiently and honestly. By doing this and continually updating them, you will generally avoid any surprises and stress. Normally, this person is the starting point of your inner circle or your "mastermind group" as Napoleon Hill (Author and Motivational Speaker) calls it.

The following quote is from John Maxwell (Leadership Expert and Author) from "Six Simple Rules for Life", "Rule #1: Put Family first. Lots of leaders give lip service to putting family first, but they don't actually practice giving their spouse or kids top priority. What does it mean to put family first? For me, it involves redefining success. I do not measure my success in terms of career accomplishments. For me, success is when those closest to me love and respect me the most. Practically speaking, I make sure to schedule time with loved ones before setting my work calendar. It's far more important for me to give prime time to my family than to "get ahead" by working overtime."

Chapter Summary

Most likely, one of the reasons why you wish to be financial independent is to provide for your family. This will be a futile endeavor, if in the process we lose their respect and love because of too much time spent chasing the dollar. We must have a balance between our financial goals and family. Put family first and when you are there be there. These simple instructions will alleviate stress and set your priorities.

Below is your action list for this chapter;
1. Schedule family time first and organize your other activities around this.
2. Make your other half the first member of your mastermind group. Explain in detail what you are trying to do and how you propose to do it. You need their approval and support.

One of your goals may be to become a millionaire and your why may be to provide for your family. The second reason, which is also the title of the book, is discussed in the next chapter.

Chapter Forty Four – Do It For What You Become

Becoming a millionaire may be the goal you have set for yourself but more importantly, the byproduct of embarking on this path is the person you will become through personal development. Jim Rohn (Philosopher and Motivational Speaker) said it best, "One day, my mentor, Mr. Shoaff said, Jim, if you want to be wealthy and happy, learn this lesson well: Learn to work harder on yourself than you do on your job. Since that time I've been working on my own personal development. And I must admit that this has been the most challenging assignment of all. This business of personal development lasts a lifetime. You see, **what you become is far more important than what you get**. The important question to ask on the job is not, "What am I getting?" Instead you should ask, "What am I becoming?"

The process of trying to achieve your goals in turn changes you and your character. Improving yourself is the key to attracting those things that you want. It is never too late to begin this transformation. Another quote from Jim Rohn asks four profound questions, "Why, Why Not, Why Not Me and Why Not Now." You are the author of your own destiny. Begin your path now, to personal development and the achievement of your goals. **Do it for what you become and do it now!**

Chapter Forty Five – Your Financial House

Throughout this book we have referred to putting your financial house in order. This chapter is meant to summarize the building blocks of wealth in a somewhat logical order. Following the outline will provide you with a path to financial independence. Financial independence can mean different things to different people. For our purposes, we will use the measuring stick of achieving one million dollars of net worth.

1. Before you begin to put your financial house in order, you must determine and commit to paper, your goals. **Remember, if you fail to plan, you are planning to fail.**

2. Next, on the list, is to write up a will. This should be updated as a minimum every two years or anytime a major change occurs in your circumstances.

3. If you have dependants that rely on you for support, obtain term life insurance.

4. Begin reducing debt. Concentrate on the bad debt that costs you the most in interest and work down the line.

5. Establish an emergency fund. Contribute to this fund until you have at least three months worth of your current income.

6. **Pay Yourself First!** Start with whatever you can but try to make the minimum 10% of any money that comes in. You may have to adjust the percentage rate based on the stage of life

you are in. For example, if you are 18 years of age, you can start with 10%. If you are 50, you have to contribute quite a bit more to achieve your goals. Regardless of where you start, as you become used to contributing and circumstances change, increase your percentage.

7. Use your pay yourself account to maximize your annual contributions to Registered Retirement Savings Plans and Tax Free Savings Accounts. Use dollar cost averaging by contributing monthly to these registered plans. With limited knowledge start by investing in Mutual Funds, Exchange Traded Funds or Segregated Funds, with an emphasis on the latter.

8. Once we have maximized the registered plans and gained experience and knowledge, invest any excess funds into the other investments mentioned in the book. Keep in mind your goals and your allowance for risk.

The next chapter describes your new routine.

Chapter Forty Six – The Routine

Throughout the book, it has been reinforced, that to reach lofty financial goals will require effort, education, discipline and time. The following list includes assignments that you should perform every day.

Daily Tasks

1. Every morning when you wake up <u>read</u> (until committed to memory) Tom Hopkin's (Sales Great and Motivator),

"Morning Mental Workout

I will win. Why? I'll tell you why – because I have faith, courage, and enthusiasm!
Today, I will meet the right people in the right place at the right time for the betterment of all.
I see opportunity in every challenge.
I'm terrific at remembering names and faces.
When I fail, I only look at what I did right.
I never take advice from anyone more messed up than I am.
I turn negative thoughts into positive ones whenever they occur.
I am a winner, a contributor, and an achiever. I believe in me!
Chants
I'm alive! I'm awake! And I feel great!

I feel good. I feel fine. I feel this way all the time!"

2. Read one hour per day non-fiction publications on investing, motivational, your job or anything business related.
3. 15 minutes per day, sit for ideas.
4. Set up automobile university and anytime you are in your vehicle listen to educational or motivational programs.
5. Maintain a journal and make entries just before going to sleep. Summarize what was done today in regards to progress on your goals, ideas and achievements.
6. Your journal should also contain your goals, read them over and peruse your vision board.
7. Don't forget at some time during the day do your research. This can be done during your reading hour, but don't consume the whole hour with research.
8. On the physical side of things, set aside one hour per day to exercise. To begin with, you may not use the entire hour for actual exercise. The remainder could involve planning or studying various methods.

You may ask where are you to find the time to do all this. Wake up earlier, watch less television or change your life style. Remember, this is not a get rich quick scheme. It will require effort, time and discipline to get to your goals. Focus on your goals everyday and you will achieve whatever you desire. The purpose of this book is to get you started in the right direction but without your effort, nothing will change.

The last chapter lists suggested books to read and media programs to use. These carry an enormous amount of valuable information to assist you on your path.

Chapter Forty Seven – Books and Media Lists

Charles "Tremendous" Jones (Author, Motivational Speaker and Comedian) states, "You will be the same person in five years as you are today, except for the people you meet and the books you read." This chapter is split into two sections. The first section is a list of books that can be read during your reading hour and the second section is a list of CD programs for automobile university. These books and CD programs will assist you in achieving your goals.

Happy reading and listening … I hope that these books and programs will help you as much as they have helped me!

Recommended Books (alphabetically listed)
Titles with Asterisks (*) Read First

*"Acres of Diamonds" by Russell H. Conwell

"Develop the Leader Within" by John Maxwell

"Endless Referrals" by Bob Burg

"Go for No" by Richard Fenton & Andrea Waltz

"How to Master the Art of Selling" by Tom Hopkins

"Life is a Series of Presentations" by Tony Jeary

"Over the Top" by Zig Ziglar

*"Rich Dad Poor Dad" by Robert Kiyosaki

"Sales Bible" by Jeffrey Gitomer

*"Stock Investing for Canadians for Dummies" by Andrew Dagys & Paul Mladjenovic

"The Automatic Millionaire" by David Bach

*"The Fireman and the Waitress" by Dessa Kaspardlov

"The Five Major Pieces to the Life Puzzle" by Jim Rohn

"The Millionaire Next Door" by Thomas Stanley & William Danko

"The One Minute Millionaire" by Mark Hansen & Robert Allen

*"The Richest Man in Babylon" by George Clason

"The 7 Habits of Highly Effective People" by Stephen Covey

"The Wealthy Barber" by David Chilton

*"Think and Grow Rich" by Napoleon Hill

"Trump the Art of the Deal" by Donald Trump

"Who Moved My Cheese" by Dr. Spencer Johnson

Also read **biographies** and auto biographies like:

"Sam Walton Made in America" by Sam Walton with John Huey.

Programs for Automobile University

"How to Stay Motivated (Goals)" by Zig Ziglar

"Lead the Field" by Earl Nightingale

"Secrets of the Millionaire Mind" by T. Harv Eker

"See You at the Top" by Zig Ziglar

"The Art of Exceptional Living" by Jim Rohn

"The Science of Personal Achievement" by Napoleon Hill

"The Weekend Millionaire's Real Estate Investing Program" by Mike Summey & Roger Dawson

A great **movie** to get, watch and learn from is:

"The Ultimate Gift".

Epilogue

With an eye on the future!

So you've made it, you now have one million net worth, what's next?

Before you actually achieved a million net worth, you should have adjusted or updated your goals. The next logical goal would be to achieve a million net worth in cash or near cash. This means to obtain a net worth of a million dollars and in the determination exclude assets that are not liquid such as collectibles or real estate etc. This does not mean to convert all your assets to cash, it means to accumulate more cash or near cash assets until you've reach that point.

In future books look for an expansion of the concepts and ideas presented. In addition you will find the following topics; "A Great Conversationalist", "Make Yourself Lucky" and "Negotiation".

Until then, I wish you the best of success in your endeavors and sincerely hope that this book has helped to increase your wealth and enhance your life.

Appendix

"I serve to enhance people's lives and promote their well being"

The author is available for seminars and personal financial planning. He welcomes any success stories you may have to share as a result of reading this book.

If you wish to obtain referrals, on specific organizations that the author has used in his personal quest to achieving his goals, send an email with your request.

Contact Information:

Email: piemar.promotions@gmail.com

Mail: P.O. Box 3035
        Fort Saskatchewan, Alberta
        T8L-2T1 CANADA